*"I am thankful to God for the faithful life and m~~~~~~~~ ~~~
Terry Virgo."*
– Dr Wayne Grudem, Researc~~ ~~~~~~~~~~~~~~~~~~s,
Phoenix Seminary, Arizona, USA

*"No one is better suited to ~~~~~~~~~~~~~~~~~~~~~~~~~~~~~~
the power of the Holy Spirit than Terry Virgo. This book will
challenge you, perhaps even shock you, but most of all it will
instruct you in what it means to experience the convergent force
of both Word and Spirit."*
– Sam Storms, Bridgeway Church, Oklahoma

*"Without the release of the Spirit believers will live defeated lives,
churches will be dead, and the Great Commission will not be
fulfilled. Terry Virgo has written a truly exceptional book that is
biblically sound, doctrinally consistent, and easily understood.
I predict this is going to have a huge impact."*
– Bob Roberts, Jr, Senior Pastor, NorthWood Church, Keller, Texas

*"The Spirit-Filled Church is 'vintage Virgo' – reflecting the godly
mind of one of God's generals. It rings of Terry's innovative
thinking from cover to cover, a word designed to stimulate and
teach us to think, to be filled afresh with the Holy Spirit, to seek
God and glorify him. It could be the book for which Terry will be
best remembered."*
– Dr R. T. Kendall, former Minister of Westminster Chapel (1977–2002)

*"Magnificent! Our churches should offer everyone a shop-front
window display of Christ's glorious kingdom! Such profound
biblical wisdom, uniting truth and power, can totally transform
sick churches today. This book's a God-send."*
– Greg Haslam, Pastor, Westminster Chapel, London

"As an observer of churches, I see a growing influence of global charismatic networks with apostolic impulse. If you want to understand this growing movement, this book is a must read."
– **Ed Stetzer,** www.edstetzer.com

"If you want to see a church that is truly Word-based and Spirit-filled, then this book is for you. Terry's lifelong experience of leading Newfrontiers gives him not only the right but also the resources to show us how to be a more Spirit-empowered, mission-shaped church. This book contains priceless wisdom from a true spiritual father. It inspires and instructs in equal measure and is a vital ingredient in Terry's massive legacy to the British and global churches."
– **Dr Mark Stibbe,** Founder and Leader of the Father's House Trust

"This is Terry at his best and a wonderful summary of the key truths that have blessed so many lives and churches. Read and be inspired!"
– **Dr David Smith,** KingsGate Community Church

"After overseeing the planting of more than seven hundred churches and giving his life to lovingly serving one of those local churches, my friend Terry Virgo has published a book on the church. Every church leader can and should learn from his humble, biblical, and practical wisdom."
– **Mark Driscoll,** Mars Hill Church, Seattle

"Through his breakthrough leadership, Terry Virgo has influenced a whole generation. He has pioneered and invented ways of bringing the kingdom of God to be incarnated in brand new 'spirit-filled' church communities all around the world. His care for truth is matched by a generosity of spirit that many outside his movement have benefitted from. His latest book is sure to do good to all who read it, so that they in turn may do good to others."
– **Charlie Cleverly,** Rector of St Aldates Oxford

TERRY
VIRGO

THE
SPIRIT-FILLED
CHURCH

FINDING
YOUR PLACE
IN GOD'S
PURPOSE

MONARCH
BOOKS
Oxford, UK & Grand Rapids, Michigan, USA

Published by Monarch Books
an imprint of
Lion Hudson plc
Wilkinson House, Jordan Hill Road,
Oxford OX2 8DR, England
Email: monarch@lionhudson.com
www.lionhudson.com/monarch

ISBN 978 0 85721 049 4 (print)
ISBN 978 0 85721 134 7 (epub)
ISBN 978 0 85721 133 0 (Kindle)
ISBN 978 0 85721 135 4 (PDF)

First edition 2011

A catalogue record for this book is available from the British Library.

Printed and bound in the UK, October 2012, LH26

For Nigel Ring, ever grateful to God for your friendship, loyalty, personal integrity, pursuit of excellence, phenomenal work rate and so much more; only God knows my profound indebtedness to you over these many years of partnership in the gospel.

CONTENTS

Foreword		8
Acknowledgments		10
Introduction		11
1.	You shall receive power	13
2.	I will be with you a little longer	20
3.	He will baptize you with the Holy Spirit	29
4.	Empowered by the Spirit and the word	39
5.	Healings and miracles, signs and wonders	48
6.	Transforming grace	56
7.	Worship in spirit and truth	65
8.	Consider yourself one of the family	76
9.	Empowering the poor	89
10.	Shepherds after my own heart	98
11.	Churches that pray	105
12.	A prophetic people	112
13.	The crucial role of leadership	122
14.	The church through an apostle's eyes	137
15.	The work of an apostle	145
Bibliography		158

FOREWORD

Jesus promised that He would build His church. But He commissioned His disciples to go into the world, without Him. Despite Jesus' return to heaven the church spread faster and became larger than any other movement in history. This was not due to the managerial skills and strategies of uneducated fishermen.

The disciples were not actually alone. Because of His death, resurrection and ascension, Jesus sent the Holy Spirit to work in them in many remarkable ways. He was indeed continuing His work.

Nothing stated above is in any way controversial. Yet many today do not expect Christians to be conscious of the Holy Spirit's activity. When He is mentioned it tends to be concerning His often hidden work in conversion.

The 21st-century Western church is struggling. We are under attack due to the growth of aggressive secularism. Established churches are shrinking at alarming rates. We might be tempted to conclude that the gates of hell are prevailing.

What hope is there? Will church management techniques save us? Will fancy websites inevitably produce growth? Should we be selecting the best entrepreneurs as our pastors?

The Apostle Paul would say to us, "are you so foolish? After beginning with the Spirit, are you now trying to attain your goal by human effort?" (Galatians 3:3, NIV)

Because the Holy Spirit initiated our Christian lives, and birthed the Church, we need Him to complete the task. We must go beyond a mere theological acceptance of His work and pursue His power today.

This is a radical book that may demolish many of your current beliefs about the church. Its author has been convinced for decades that the church can resemble the model described in Acts. These are not the untested ideas of a young man who thinks he has all the answers. Terry Virgo has devoted his life to embracing both the Spirit's power and the rock-solid foundation of the Scriptures. He founded a global movement of over 800 vibrant, grace-rooted, Spirit-filled churches in more than 60 nations, and on every continent.

All over the world in spontaneous groups that are often unaware of each other, people are embracing similar ideas. The growing global church is very conscious of being Spirit-filled. If you live where the power of evil spirits is very evident, you need a God who is alive and active. As cultural Christianity recedes, it is not just secularism that is seeking to replace it. Many in the West are seeking spiritual reality. Will they find it in your church? Or will they reject Christianity as powerless and search elsewhere?

I pray that this book will fuel a hunger in your soul to pursue a greater awareness of the Holy Spirit's presence. I ask this, not only that you will be personally blessed, happier, and more assured of your faith. I ask because there is no greater need in the world today than for an army of people filled with the Spirit.

Adrian Warnock
Author, *Raised With Christ – How the Resurrection Changes Everything*

ACKNOWLEDGMENTS

I owe a debt of gratitude to so many who have helped me on my way in terms of inspiring values and vision for *The Spirit-Filled Church*.

I particularly want to thank the members of Church of Christ the King in Brighton for their support, love and prayerful encouragement and also all my dear brothers and sisters in the wider *Newfrontiers* family scattered in many nations around the world.

Janis Peters, my secretary, deserves special praise for her constant enthusiasm and kindness in typing and re-typing the manuscript of the book. Her excellent attitude and skills have combined to complete the work that is before you now.

INTRODUCTION

I am sometimes asked if I am a conservative evangelical. My reply is that it depends what you mean by "conservative". If by conservative you mean "cautious", then I guess I am not, but if you mean that as an evangelical I want to conserve biblical Christianity, I most certainly am.

I have occasionally been asked to fill in a questionnaire in which I am required to state whether I am a charismatic or Reformed evangelical Christian. I don't want to confuse people but, like the apostle Paul, I aim to be both! I believe in an awesome, sovereign God and see no reason to suppose that spiritual gifts as described in the New Testament have been withdrawn from the church.

It is my conviction that local churches hold the key to world evangelization. The early apostles, told to go and make disciples, instinctively went and planted churches where discipleship could take place in a community of love cared for by called and gifted elders. The promised outpouring of the Holy Spirit galvanized them into action. Soon they gained the reputation that they were turning the world upside down!

The gospel of the grace of God set people free and formed them into communities of believers shaped by apostolic doctrine and energized by God's empowering presence. It is my conviction that the model of the early church still holds the key to 21st-century world evangelization.

The worldview of the average man or woman in the West has been radically transformed in the past century, making the modern mission field look very similar to the one which Paul and the early apostles encountered as they travelled among the nations. Christendom, with all its vague endorsement of Christian values, has gone. Secularism rules, sometimes urged on by aggressive atheism. The church has to rediscover its early zeal, power and gospel clarity. Local churches will need to be seen as relevant to this generation, providing genuine answers, not merely religious platitudes.

A fragmented society, characterized by individualism and loneliness, needs to discover churches in which groups of people have discovered genuine answers, know how to relate in love and trust, and have found God in terms that can be understood and embraced with joy.

Can God be known? Can He be experienced? Are there people on the planet who are genuinely experiencing Him? Few enquirers into Christianity anticipate that they will meet such people. They tend to regard us as merely religious types who have opted out from the real world and embraced a pre-set formula of rules and regulations. Most are unaware of churches filled with people who themselves were formerly unbelievers but who have encountered God, experienced the lavish outpouring of His Spirit and been built into loving communities.

May God help us to continue to make the gospel known to our generation and build relevant churches for His great glory. The following chapters highlight some experiences and biblical principles which have been impressed upon me over the last few decades and which have resulted in the planting of hundreds of churches in many nations.

CHAPTER 1

YOU SHALL RECEIVE POWER

Ignoring someone's final instructions would not be smart, especially if that person holds all authority in heaven and earth. Before ascending into heaven Jesus told His disciples, "you will receive power when the Holy Spirit has come upon you; and you shall be My witnesses both in Jerusalem, and in all Judea and Samaria, and even to the remotest part of the earth" (Acts 1:8).

For Jesus' followers, with their Jewish background, the concept of "receiving power" and "the Spirit coming upon" people was no mystery. They would have known their sacred Scriptures and been familiar with the stories of Israel's famous heroes such as Gideon, Samson, Saul and David, whose lives were dramatically transformed when the Holy Spirit came upon them. They knew how the seventy received some of the Spirit that had rested upon Moses, and Joshua was empowered by the Spirit when Moses laid his hands on him.

Fearful Gideon, called by God to a mammoth and frightening task, regarded himself as an irrelevant son of an irrelevant father and by no means a courageous military leader. When he was hidden away in a cave, safe from marauding enemies, God called and commissioned him. He also clothed him with the Holy Spirit's power, as a result of which he became a genuinely charismatic leader, gathering Israel and inspiring a tiny, outnumbered army into a famous victory, his secret being the transformation that took place when the Spirit came upon him (Judges 6:34).

David's phenomenal success was rooted in a secret encounter with

Samuel the prophet, who anointed him with oil, "and the Spirit of the Lord came mightily upon David from that day forward" (1 Samuel 16:13).

Elisha knew that if he were to continue what Elijah had started, he must have the same Spirit that rested on his master; without that powerful anointing it would be impossible. Likewise, Peter and the apostles must have recognized that if they were to carry on where Jesus had stopped, they would need similar power.

WHAT ABOUT US?

As a young Christian this was precisely the question that I asked. All too aware of my serious personal limitations, I was deeply conscious of my own need of power to serve God. The Scriptures made plain how timid Peter, who denied his Lord, was amazingly transformed by the coming of the Holy Spirit on him. His fears were banished; he became bold and fearless in proclaiming the gospel. I longed for the same. Could I receive the Spirit like Peter did? Could I be clothed with power and transformed like Gideon had been?

I developed a growing and increasingly insistent thirst that if there was an experience of the Holy Spirit that would make Jesus more real and more obviously present, and that would set me free from my inhibitions and reluctance, I wanted it! Too often I had missed opportunities to bear witness to Christ and be public about my personal commitment to Him.

Some work colleagues and friends knew that I was a church-goer but none knew that I believed from the depths of my heart that Jesus Christ was God's Son, that I was personally certain my sins were forgiven, and that I knew I had eternal life. I found no liberty at all to speak to people about things that really mattered. If I could know the kind of release that Peter and the apostles enjoyed, I was eager to find it for myself. Perhaps you find yourself in the same position.

The question that still arises for many Christians is, "Where do I fit into all this?" Am I automatically Spirit-filled at my conversion or do I have to wait for an endowment of the Spirit, as the disciples did in early Acts? As a young Christian I was thoroughly perplexed.

I read all the books on the subject that I could lay my hands on, and concluded that if respected men like John Stott and Dr Martyn Lloyd-Jones (both great heroes of mine) could not agree about it, there was very little hope that I would work it out. I was, however, personally persuaded that I needed power from God. I tried to pray about it by myself and tried to receive the experience of the Spirit's empowering by faith. I sometimes was able to convince myself that something had happened, but gradually it all drained away and I had to admit the depressing truth that I was no different from before.

For me, the whole thing came to a head one Sunday afternoon. I had been leading a Bible Study for the young people at our church, and I decided to get some fresh air before the evening service. I headed for Brighton on the English coast, not far from where I lived. In the area known as the Fish Market I encountered an embarrassing spectacle. Surrounded by a crowd of laughing people and assailed by assorted coins and cigarette packets, two elderly ladies were preaching the gospel. The whole scene, with its Bible text banners, the reedy voices of the old ladies, the mocking crowd, filled me with shame.

"Why does it have to be like this?" I thought.

"You are ashamed because these are old ladies," came the answer. "In the Bible I called vigorous young men to do this sort of thing. But these old ladies are willing to do it. Are you?"

"Lord, I would rather die than stand in the open air like that," I honestly replied.

Just then I was aware of two men in front of me and overheard one say, "Look at those old fools! Why can't they keep their religion to themselves? Why don't they keep it in their churches?"

Again I heard a voice inside me: "If you can't stand up and preach, at least you can own me to these two men. Tell them that you are a Christian."

I recoiled even from this prospect. I had just spoken to Christians at a Bible Study with great confidence but I had never been free to talk to the unconverted about Jesus. I felt ashamed of my cowardice. Miserable, I rushed home, got on my knees and cried out to God that I must be filled with the Spirit. Jesus said, "If anyone is thirsty, let him come to Me and drink. He who believes in Me, as the Scripture said, 'From his innermost being will flow rivers of living water'" (John 7:37–38). God has ways of making us thirsty! I was desperate!

The next day, when I arrived at my office in London, I phoned a friend with whom I often had lunch. "Derek," I said, "I must see you. Can we meet at lunchtime?" He readily agreed. I knew there was something different about Derek. Often we shared a table with others in a café; he would talk with them about Christ and give them a tract. While I squirmed, he would talk freely about the Lord. I found it all so embarrassing. I hated his freedom while at the same time longing for it with all my heart. I told him how I felt, adding, "I must have what you've got." He invited me to his church on the following Sunday saying that someone there would pray for me to be baptized with the Holy Spirit.

A LIFE-CHANGING DAY

The following weekend found me travelling to London to stay with Derek. On the Saturday evening I met some of the young people from his church. They were going on a bus trip to take part in a meeting at another church. Never had I seen such a zealous, vital group. Several were invited by their leader to stand up and give their testimonies without any prior warning or preparation. It was magnificent. The young people I was used to would need a few weeks' notice for this sort of thing and even then would have read from notes.

For the first time in my life I heard someone speak in tongues during the course of a meeting and then, to my astonishment, one of the young Londoners who had been laughing and joking on the coach earlier gave an interpretation. It was amazing. Everything seemed to be in a different league from anything I had ever encountered, but I knew that this was what I wanted.

The next afternoon I was taken to a special meeting for those who wanted to be baptized in the Holy Spirit. The previous day we had been fasting and praying together about my need to be filled with the Spirit, and Derek had prophesied. I had never heard this gift before but I received it as if God Himself was speaking. "My little sheep," he said, "keep very close to me and I will lead you to living waters and give you your heart's desire." Having heard the promise, I had no doubt that God was going to fill me with His Holy Spirit.

The pastor moved along the line, praying for each one in turn to be filled with the Spirit. Eventually he came to me and laid his hands on my head. I felt nothing at all! All my expectations and hopes were shattered.

When the pastor finished praying for me and left the room, the people around me said, "Well, praise the Lord, then." Everyone in the room was praising God except me, but I refused to join in. How could I praise the Lord when nothing had happened? I wanted something real! I was then shown from the Bible the place of faith in all our dealings with God. I saw that I had done all that I could. I had come to God; hands had been laid upon me; I must now believe Him. Certainly I had come expecting to receive. I had arrived at this moment full of faith. So I turned back to God and quietly thanked Him.

That did not satisfy my friends, however. "Come on, Terry," they encouraged me. "Praise God in tongues." I longed to be able to do just that, but how? "Just begin to speak!" they told me. They reminded me that it was not God who spoke in tongues on the Day of Pentecost, but that the disciples themselves spoke in other tongues as the Spirit gave them utterance (Acts 2:4). It all sounded most unsatisfactory to me, but, in spite of all my arguments, my friends prevailed. I spoke some sounds, some syllables. Even as I did so a thousand voices in my mind were mocking me, telling me that I was making it all up. I stopped, but my friends encouraged me to carry on. I did so, pressing on and battling against the doubts that were flooding my mind.

Through all these doubts, I heard my friend's fiancée speak. "You know, you're very clever, Terry, if you are making all this up. You have been doing it for ages."

We all laughed together and the tension was broken. I realized how worried I had become about it all; how self-defeating it was to get so intense. As I relaxed and continued to speak in tongues it was as if a flood of the Holy Spirit went right through me. I found myself not only speaking freely in tongues but also calling out to God in the most loving and intimate terms that I could imagine. God was right here in my heart! His love was absolutely overflowing in me! I truly loved Him like never before.

The meeting was now over and the main church service was about to start, but I didn't want to stop this wonderful new experience with its amazing sense of the intimacy of God's presence right inside me! I sat in the back row of the very large church building, while others were all in the front half, put my hand over my mouth so that I would not disturb anybody and spoke in tongues throughout the whole service. I had been a Christian for six years and had never doubted my salvation but had never known anything like it! God was so present! This was joy unspeakable and full of glory!

"ABBA! FATHER!"

In Paul's words, "Because you are sons, God has sent forth the Spirit of His Son into our hearts, crying, 'Abba! Father!'" (Galatians 4:6). As Douglas Moo says, commenting on Romans 8:15: "In using the verb 'crying out', Paul stresses that our awareness of God as Father comes not from rational consideration or from external testimony alone, but from a truth deeply felt and intensely experienced" (Douglas Moo, *The Epistle to the Romans*, The New International Commentary on the New Testament, Eerdmans, 1996). For me this was certainly a truth being "deeply felt and intensely experienced". I had never felt or experienced such a thing before!

Within a short space of time I had the great privilege of sharing my testimony with the young people from the Baptist church to which I belonged in Hove and, with the pastor's encouragement, laid hands on many of them, whereupon they entered enthusiastically into a similar experience. Dr Martyn Lloyd-Jones wrote: "The baptism with the Spirit is always associated primarily and specifically with witness and testimony and service" (Dr Martyn Lloyd-Jones, *Joy Unspeakable*, Kingsway, 1984).

In the weeks that followed, I and several of those young people regularly spent our Sunday afternoons at Brighton's Fish Market where we stood together and sang, after which I stood on a box and began to preach on that same seafront to the passing crowds. Things had become dramatically different. I was actually doing what I had always regarded as impossible. The Holy Spirit had set me free.

CHAPTER 2

I WILL BE WITH YOU A LITTLE LONGER

Having left everything to follow Jesus, Peter and his friends heard some desperately alarming words: "My children, I will be with you only a little longer…" (John 13:33 NIV). What on earth did He mean? Was He going away? How could that be? He had invited men to follow Him. He chose twelve simply "so that they would be with Him" (Mark 3:14). That was the call – being with Him! Jesus did not invite people to attend the temple or synagogue. Their discipleship was not to be expressed simply by attending meetings. His invitation was clear, namely to be with Him!

Paul claimed, "we do not preach ourselves" (2 Corinthians 4:5). Not so Jesus. He constantly preached Himself: "I am the good shepherd… I am the door… I am the true vine… I am the way, the truth and the life… I am the light of the world… I am the bread of life." He was not afraid to present Himself as the answer. "Come to me" was His invitation. Peter had left everything with the clear intention of being with Him. Now He was going away. Where did that leave Peter and the others?

THE PRESENCE OF GOD

The Jewish people enjoyed a unique privilege; God was with them, distinguishing them from every other nation. Moses, while looking after a few sheep, suddenly saw a bush burning but not being consumed. Drawing near, he heard God calling him by name. Holy ground demanded that his feet should lose their sandals. Scaring him half to death, a voice spoke, calling him by name and telling him to go to Egypt and bring the 2 million Israelites back to this spot. If a bush burned for Moses, the whole mountain burst into life for the Israelite nation. Thunder, lightning, a glory cloud, a trumpet and a voice that they all heard (Exodus 19:18–19; Deuteronomy 4:33).

No nation was ever so privileged. God went with them! A cloud of glory led them by day and night. At one point, due to their backsliding, God threatened to withdraw, but Moses was insistent: "If Your presence does not go with us, do not lead us up from here… Is it not by Your going with us, so that we, I and Your people, may be distinguished from all the other people who are upon the face of the earth?" (Exodus 33:15–16).

This was their claim to fame – a people distinguished by the manifest presence of God! He was so keen to be among them that He gave them instructions for a special tent to be made: "Let them construct a sanctuary for Me, that I may dwell among them" (Exodus 25:8). Not content to stay on the mountaintop, God wanted His own tent among theirs. "Moses finished the work. Then the cloud covered the tent of meeting, and the glory of the Lord filled the tabernacle" (Exodus 40:33–34). God's presence had arrived! The people regularly watched the cloud of glory come down on the tent.

NO LONGER A CLOUD, BUT A PERSON

Our New Testament starts with an even more remarkable announcement. A child will be born named Immanuel, or "God with us" (Matthew 1:23). Or, to use John's language, "the Word became flesh, and dwelt among us" (John 1:14). Literally, He "tabernacled" among us. He pitched His tent among men.

Now the glory of God's presence was no longer in a phenomenal glowing cloud of fire but in a man – an accessible person. Later, on reflection, John said, "we saw His glory" (John 1:14).

In his prologue, John introduced his gospel by telling us that "No one has seen God at any time". This One from "the bosom of the Father" has explained Him (John 1:18) – or made Him known. Literally, He provided the "exegesis". We preachers take a text and try to give the exegesis. We explain what it means. John 1:18 tells us that Jesus came to give us the exegesis of the Father.

The writer to the Hebrews says (Hebrews 1:3) that God spoke in several ways in the past but in these last days God has spoken to us in His Son, who is "the radiance of His glory and the exact representation of His nature". He is the outshining radiance of God. No man has seen God at any time. Just as we cannot gaze directly at the sun, but can often see magnificent rays of sunlight pouring through gaps in the clouds, so we cannot see God but we can know Him through the One who has come to us where we are. The sun's rays are the outshining of the sun. They are the sun coming to us in ways that it is possible for us to see. Jesus came to man radiating the presence of God.

Hebrews also says that Jesus is the exact representation of God's nature. He perfectly represented God. There was no blemish that would mislead us. Jesus could say to Philip when the latter pleaded, "show us the Father", "He who has seen Me has seen the Father" (John 14:9). People may hazard guesses, or project their theories about God, but we have a God just like Jesus. Although he taught his disciples to pray what we call "the Lord's prayer", he never actually prayed it. He never needed to ask for forgiveness. He never sinned. He was innocent and spotless, a perfect likeness.

LIVING DAILY WITH GOD

Looking at Jesus, you see God perfectly represented in terms that can be understood. God's attitudes to children, to harlots, to scared disciples, to religious bigots and hypocrites are perfectly revealed through the words and actions of the Lord Jesus, without any discrepancy!

The coming of Jesus of Nazareth was no less than the Word becoming flesh and dwelling among us. John said, "what we have heard, what we have seen with our eyes, what we have looked at and touched with our hands…" (1 John 1:1). One can imagine John repeatedly looking at his own hands as he wrote such words.

"I saw Him and touched Him and even leaned on Him as we ate together. I leaned on God! I daily watched Him do amazing miracles and healings. I saw Him transform lives and even transform whole towns, healing all who were there. I listened to every word. I talked to Him, asking Him questions every day. I left everything in order to be with Him. Every day was truly awesome; it was breath-taking.

"You cannot imagine what it was like to be around Jesus day after day. One day, for instance, Jesus climbed a mountain. We disciples went with him but thousands followed, bringing all the lame, crippled, blind, mute and others. All day Jesus healed and taught them. We stayed there, slept through the night and continued through two more days. In the end there were 4,000 men, plus women and children with us, and no one remained sick. Finally, he supernaturally broke a few loaves and we fed everybody there!

"God came to a mountain to be with thousands of people, healed every one and fed them all. Each day we woke and wondered, what will He do today? Day after day we lived with Him.

"But one day He said, 'I am with you a little while longer.' What could He mean? He had become my life! He was everything! Now He was going to leave us."

HE'S GONE

What was the church going to become? A group of people gathering around a fading memory of what it was like to have God with them? "Quick! Let's write down as much as we can remember of what He said. But He's gone!"

Their daily experience of being with Christ was so wonderful. What would it be like to live without Him? He electrified their days with His presence. How could they exist bereft of Him? This would be a bereavement of untold agony.

Into their despair and despondency, Jesus spoke words that offered new hope: "I will not leave you as orphans; I will come to you" (John 14:18). I can imagine Peter thinking, "Oh, thank God! He's coming back. It's OK, guys – he's coming back! Lord, you must not scare us like that again! I thought you really meant you were going away! How could I return to a life without you?"

But what did "I will come to you" mean? How would He come?

I sometimes wonder if we are wise when we offer John's Gospel to enquirers and seekers after God. It seems a common practice: "If you are interested in Christianity, read John's Gospel." Surely it's the most enigmatic and difficult of the gospels. Within a few chapters the new birth is introduced to the baffled Nicodemus, who asks if he must re-enter his mother's womb. Chapter 4 introduces the confusing conversation at the well with the Samaritan woman. What kind of water is He talking about? By chapter 6 Jesus is telling people they must eat His flesh and drink His blood. John's Gospel is a difficult book!

In John 14–16, Jesus also begins to introduce one of the greatest mysteries of the Christian faith, namely the Trinity. This will not all be plain sailing!

NOT LEFT AS ORPHANS

When Jesus says, "I will not leave you orphans, I will come to you," he has been understood by commentators in a number of ways. Bishop Westcott's classic commentary says:

> *The fulfilment of the promise began at the resurrection, when Christ's humanity was glorified; and the promise was potentially completed at Pentecost. The life of the church is the realisation of the Pentecostal coming of the Lord, which is to be crowned by His coming in judgment. No one specific application of the phrase exhausts its meaning.*
>
> **(Westcott, *The Gospel According to St John*, James Clarke & Co, 1958)**

In other words, Bishop Westcott tells us there are three possible ways of understanding the promise "I will come to you". It could either be the breath-taking resurrection appearances, or the fact that ultimately Christ will return to the earth. He also states, "The promise was potentially completed at Pentecost." My personal understanding would be to plump for the Pentecostal coming.

William Hendriksen says, "What Jesus means is, 'My departure will not be like that of a father whose children are left as orphans when he dies. In the Spirit I am myself coming back to you.'… When the Spirit is poured out, Christ truly returns." Hendriksen, the conservative Reformed scholar, puts all his eggs in that particular basket, arguing that "Thus only can it be explained that the disciples are not left orphans" (William Hendriksen, *The Gospel of John*, Banner of Truth, 1959).

Surely he has it right. Surely the glorious resurrection appearances, with all their comfort and unspeakable joy, do not ultimately fulfil the promise that they would not be left orphans, because in forty days' time Jesus would disappear once again, being taken up into the cloud. Once again they would be without Him.

Also, the promise of the Lord's return taking place in a few thousand years' time is not of great comfort to a group of men who have been told to go and tell the world about Jesus. It is wonderful to know that Jesus will come again, finally establish His glorious kingdom and usher in a new earth and new heavens, but this is no answer for the here and now! I agree with William Hendriksen.

Jesus is trying to prepare His disciples for a remarkable future of gospel advance, starting in Jerusalem and spreading throughout Judea, Samaria and to the ends of the earth. He wanted them confident and assured. They had expected Him to lead them into whatever messianic victories were lying ahead. Now, having said that He would only be with them a little longer, He added the comforting assurance that He wouldn't leave them as orphans – He would come to them.

BETTER FOR YOU

Jesus is about to develop the understanding of His disciples with regard to the Trinity. He is beginning to promise the coming of the

Spirit but, in the words of Hendriksen, "'In the Spirit I am myself coming back to you.'… When the Spirit is poured out, Christ truly returns."

As Christians we believe in a three-person Trinity – Father, Son and Holy Spirit. At a casual glance we might be tempted to ask, "Who or what, then, is the Spirit of Christ?"

Paul speaks in similar fashion in Galatians 4:6 when he says that because we are now fully sons through Christ's work of redemption, God has now sent "the Spirit of His Son into our hearts". Notice, Paul does not call Him the Holy Spirit on this occasion but "the Spirit of His Son". He makes a similar reference in Philippians when he refers to their prayers and "the provision of the Spirit of Jesus Christ" (Philippians 1:19) – again a clear reference to the Holy Spirit but with this different title – "the Spirit of Jesus Christ".

The Holy Spirit's coming would mean that it would be like having Jesus with them. Indeed, Jesus must have amazed them with His promise that actually it would be better for them when the Holy Spirit came. Better, not worse; superior, not inferior; surpassing their previous experience of being with Christ. They were to expect Jesus to come to them but He would not come as before, but in a new way – namely, by the Holy Spirit, and this could be anticipated with extraordinary joy and delight. What could be better?

Luke's introduction to his second account (the Acts of the Apostles) began with the telling words, "The first account I composed, Theophilus, about all that Jesus *began* to do and teach" (my italics; Acts 1:1). Surely he was implying that the second account would include what Jesus continued to do and teach. As John Stott says:

Luke's first two verses are, therefore, extremely significant. It is no exaggeration to say that they set Christianity apart from all other religions. These regard their founder as having completed his ministry during his lifetime; Luke says Jesus only began his.
(**John Stott, *The Message of Acts*, The Bible Speaks Today, IVP, 1990**)

HE ABIDES WITH YOU AND WILL
BE IN YOU

By way of explanation regarding the Holy Spirit, Jesus reminded them that they were not ignorant of the Spirit's presence. They had been in His company for three remarkable years. They had witnessed the power of the Holy Spirit in their daily experience of being with the Lord Jesus. The phenomenal miracles that had been taking place were evident proof of the Spirit's powerful activity. Preaching in Cornelius' home, Peter explained his Master's breath-taking ministry as follows: "You know of Jesus of Nazareth, how God anointed Him with the Holy Spirit and with power, and how He went about doing good and healing all who were oppressed by the devil, for God was with Him" (Acts 10:38).

Peter and the others had first-hand daily exposure to the power of the Holy Spirit. Now they could anticipate a new intimacy with the Spirit. The One who had been with them and powerfully among them was going to be in them (John 14:17).

This promise was immediately followed by the words, "I will come to you". Their new and powerful experience of the Spirit in them was to be understood as Christ coming to them in a new way. The heartbroken Mary Magdalene, devastated at the tomb because they had taken away her Lord, was overwhelmed with joy when she heard His familiar voice speak her name and saw that He was indeed alive. But she was quickly told not to cling to Him (John 20:17). From now on they would know Him in a new kind of way.

They would not be orphans and left alone. They would have an internal experience of the Holy Spirit that would be in keeping with the mighty activity of the Spirit that they had observed in Jesus' life and ministry. So in many ways the book of the Acts of the Apostles would look very much like a continuation of the gospel accounts.

Similar power would be present. Similar boldness would be observable. These "uneducated and untrained men" would astound the Jewish religious leaders, who were amazed and recognized them as having been with Jesus (Acts 4:13). From the Sanhedrin's point of view, the disciples looked frighteningly like Him in terms of power and influence.

They had isolated, crushed and destroyed one powerful preacher and miracle-worker, only to find He was being reproduced in others. No wonder Jesus had warned the apostles, before they began to proclaim His name among the nations, that they must stay in the city until they were clothed with power from on high (Luke 24:49). On the Day of Pentecost, as they burst out, apparently drunk, before an unsuspecting world, uppermost in their hearts must have been the wonderful realization, "He's back!" Their glorious Lord was manifestly among them again.

The coming of the Spirit must not be regarded as something far less than this! God's empowering presence provided the phenomenal energy of the New Testament church. He was ostensibly and spectacularly among them.

CHAPTER 3

HE WILL BAPTIZE YOU WITH THE HOLY SPIRIT

It was John the Baptist's privilege to prepare the way for the coming of Christ. He was a voice crying out. He was the Bridegroom's friend coming ahead of time to introduce the Saviour's arrival. It is recorded in every gospel and even repeated in the opening chapter of the book of Acts, "John baptized with water, but you will be baptized with the Holy Spirit not many days from now" (Acts 1:5).

John not only pointed to Christ as the Lamb of God who would take away our sin; he also highlighted the glorious truth that Jesus would baptize people in the Holy Spirit, the widespread outpouring promised in the Old Testament.

In Old Testament days isolated individuals such as prophets, priests, kings and judges were singularly blessed by their enduement of power from on high, but the prophet Joel promised a new day that would break out in world history when God would pour out His Spirit upon all flesh, male and female, young and old, accompanied by such supernatural manifestations as prophesying, seeing of visions and dreaming of dreams.

Considering the high priority that John gave in pointing to Jesus as the One who would bring this baptism, it is strange that Jesus in fact said little about the Holy Spirit's coming throughout His three years of public ministry. The gospel accounts provide only a handful of verses where Jesus draws the attention of His followers to the coming of the Spirit.

Only when the shadow of the cross begins to loom large over the disciples does Jesus draw them together in the upper room and speak in detail about the coming of the Holy Spirit. One very enigmatic statement in John 7:37–39 provides a vital key to our understanding of the Holy Spirit's coming:

> *Jesus stood and cried out, saying, "If anyone is thirsty, let him come to Me and drink. He who believes in Me, as the Scripture said, 'From his innermost being will flow rivers of living water.'" But this He spoke of the Spirit, whom those who believed in Him were to receive; for the Spirit was not yet given, because Jesus was not yet glorified.*

It would have been strange to be present on that occasion and hear the Lord's glorious invitation to come to Him and drink. If you had pressed through the crowd and got to Him, you would sadly have heard, "Not yet!" Jesus was giving an invitation but its fulfilment was definitely not yet.

Jesus Himself must first be glorified. He must first endure His own "baptism". He must endure the cross, be vindicated by the resurrection and gloriously ascend to the right hand of God before the Holy Spirit would be given, so although He offered "rivers of living water", the time was not yet.

The book of Acts provides the explanation and the only inspired report of how Jesus fulfilled His promise to His thirsty disciples. Only after He had ascended to heaven did He become the One who would baptize with the Holy Spirit. It is important for us, therefore, to look into the book of Acts and be instructed.

Sadly, some have suggested that we should not expect to receive explicit teaching from reading narrative passages. They have, therefore, taken the stance that the book of Acts is not an appropriate book for us to study as we try to discover what is meant by being baptized in the Holy Spirit. They would argue that doctrine should be drawn from "didactic" (i.e. teaching) parts of the New Testament such as the epistles. But this attitude thoroughly undermines the teaching of 2 Timothy 3:16 that all Scripture is God-breathed and is useful for teaching, rebuking, correcting and training in righteousness. Much of our Scripture is narrative and Paul explicitly argues, "these things happened to them as an example, and they were written for our instruction, upon whom the ends of the ages have come" (1 Corinthians 10:11). Paul is, therefore, declaring that narrative passages provide examples and were expressly recorded to instruct us. We therefore need to approach the book of Acts with the mindset that there are God-ordained examples which have been carefully recorded to provide the instruction that we need. As Dr Martyn Lloyd-Jones argued: "you really cannot truly interpret nor understand the teaching of the epistles unless you do so in the light of the history of Acts" (Dr Martyn Lloyd-Jones, *Joy Unspeakable*, Kingsway, 1984).

The gospels anticipate the coming of the Holy Spirit and the epistles take for granted that believers have received Him, even as they do that believers have, of course, been baptized in water. Only the book of Acts tells us what actually happened and how He came to new believers.

THE KEY TO THE BOOK OF ACTS

Many have suggested that Acts 1:8 provides the key to the book of Acts, namely: "you will receive power when the Holy Spirit has come upon you…" Frightened disciples were going to be transformed. Reluctant witnesses, shut away in an upper room, were about to be empowered, inspired and energized. God came upon them in extraordinary power, making them hardly recognizable from their previous state. Trembling Peter, for instance, who had completely denied any association with Jesus of Nazareth when questioned by onlookers, is now almost unrecognizably different. Now the Jewish leaders take note of his phenomenal boldness and are baffled as to how he and the other unlearned disciples could speak with such awesome authority.

The apostles were not only personally transformed but mightily accompanied with power from on high. They found themselves preaching with "the Holy Spirit sent from heaven" (see 1 Peter 1:12). God accompanied their preaching and "worked with them, and confirmed the word by the signs that followed" (Mark 16:20). God did not leave them to bear witness alone but was powerfully at work in partnership with them, "God also testifying with them, both by signs and wonders and by various miracles and by gifts of the Holy Spirit according to His own will" (Hebrews 2:4).

Peter, who had formerly demonstrated fear and horror when the little girl's question caught him like a rabbit transfixed by oncoming headlights, was now like a roaring lion. The day of Pentecost had fully come!

BUT WHERE DO WE FIT IN?

In many ways the experience of Jesus' contemporaries was unique. They were His followers before the cross, the resurrection and the day of Pentecost. Redemption had not been secured. Resurrection life was not yet available. Because they lived through these great events and were followers of Jesus while they were taking place, it is very difficult for us to identify with their experience. However, the book of Acts does provide plenty of illustration and instruction about how new Christians, saved after the day of Pentecost, encountered the Holy Spirit's coming.

As a young Christian, I was very confused. There seemed to be a number of different schools of thought regarding receiving the Spirit. Some simply taught that if you were a Christian you had already received the Holy Spirit, and that was that! They might add that during your Christian life you will hopefully gradually be increasingly filled with the Holy Spirit as you grow in grace and maturity.

This was the line that my own church took and I had yet to be exposed to the thunderings of Dr Martyn Lloyd-Jones when he challenged his hearers, "Got it all? Well, if you have got it all, I simply ask in the name of God why are you as you are? If you have got it all, why are you so unlike New Testament Christians? Got it all! Got it at your conversion! Well where is it, I ask?" ("Quenching the Holy Spirit", *Westminster Record*, September 1969).

Others seemed to suggest that there was more to be experienced, but there was still considerable diversity in what seemed to be on offer. Some implied that the fullness of the Holy Spirit was for the mature, or perhaps for those who had "emptied themselves out" in a specific approach to sanctification in order to receive a second blessing.

One would often hear the illustration of a glass which needs first to be emptied before it could be filled, and this was often taught in the context of a fresh step of consecration and commitment to Christ and had clear sanctification implications. Some had even developed that into a doctrine of "entire sanctification" where the encounter with the Spirit was thought to "burn up" indwelling sin and give you a pure heart. As a young Christian it clearly seemed out of reach for me.

I was also told about Pentecostals who still believed in speaking in tongues and regarded that gift as the "initial evidence" that one had been baptized in the Holy Spirit. Later the "charismatic movement" seemed to embrace the Pentecostal position, but with variations.

It was all very confusing!

The Day of Pentecost, described in Acts 2, was unique. It fulfilled a historic day in the Jewish calendar which commemorated God's faithfulness in the giving of the harvest but also celebrated the giving of the law to Moses and the people of Israel. Each year Jews, not only from Israel but from the international Diaspora, would make the journey to Jerusalem to celebrate the Feast of Pentecost.

After the memorable day recorded in Acts 2, this Old Testament feast was overshadowed by not only the phenomenal evangelistic harvest that immediately took place – 3,000 in a single day – but also by the new inward impartation of the law to the hearts of those who received (see Romans 8:3–4).

YOU SHALL RECEIVE POWER

The apostles had been told not to begin their work until they were "clothed with power from on high" (Luke 24:49). Obediently, they waited for the "promise of My Father" and were transformed by His coming. Peter stood with the eleven to declare to the amazed crowds that Christ was now vindicated and established at the right hand of God and that, as a result, the promised Holy Spirit had been received and poured forth (see Acts 2:33).

He continued by calling them to repent and be baptized in the name of Jesus Christ for the forgiveness of sins, following which they would receive the gift of the Holy Spirit (see Acts 2:38).

THE SAMARITANS

Within a short time, Philip, the only named evangelist in the New Testament, powerfully preached the gospel in Samaria. "When they believed Philip preaching the good news about the kingdom of God and the name of Jesus Christ, they were being baptized, men and women alike" (Acts 8:12). These new believers were immediately baptized, but subsequently the apostles at Jerusalem, having heard that the Samaritans had received the word of God, sent Peter and John who came and prayed for them that they might receive the Holy Spirit (Acts 8:15). For thus far "He had not yet fallen upon any of them" (Acts 8:16).

When they laid their hands on them, the Samaritans received the Holy Spirit. Their testimony would, therefore, have been that they were saved and baptized in water through Philip's gospel preaching but that some days later they received the Holy Spirit as a separate experience. As Dr Martyn Lloyd-Jones said of them, "These people were already true believers on the Lord Jesus Christ and him crucified as their Saviour. They had been baptised into his name because they had become believers, but still they were not baptised with the Holy Spirit" (Dr Martyn Lloyd-Jones, *Joy Unspeakable*, Kingsway, 1984).

"BROTHER SAUL"

Paul himself had a similar testimony. Dramatically converted on the road to Damascus, he was three days later approached by Ananias, an unknown disciple who laid hands on him, referring to him as "brother Saul", so that he might not only regain his sight but also be filled with the Holy Spirit (Acts 9:17). Plainly, according to the Scriptures, Paul was filled with the Holy Spirit three days after his famous conversion.

CORNELIUS AND FRIENDS

Acts 10 tells a remarkable story of the apostle Peter's reluctance to go to a Gentile house. God prepared him through a vivid vision of a sheet full of animals which he regarded as unclean. Initially God's command to him to rise and eat was thoroughly unacceptable to him. Following two repeats of the vision, men from Cornelius, the Roman centurion, invited him to the home of this "unclean gentile".

Upon arrival, Peter overcame his misgivings and preached the gospel of Christ in the Gentile's home. "While Peter was still speaking these words, the Holy Spirit fell upon all those who were listening to the message" (Acts 10:44). The Jewish Christians were amazed "because the gift of the Holy Spirit had been poured out on the Gentiles also. For they were hearing them speaking with tongues and exalting God" (Acts 10:45–46).

TWELVE EPHESIANS

Finally Paul arrived at the great city of Ephesus and encountered twelve men whom Acts 19:1 describes as "disciples". Having enquired about their experience, Paul discovered that they were totally ignorant about the Holy Spirit and were in fact disciples of John the Baptist whose message of repentance drew vast crowds and travelled as far as Ephesus.

Paul then led them on from John's repentance message and told them all about the Lord Jesus, as a result of which they were immediately baptized in the name of the Lord Jesus (Acts 19:5). Then, while they were perhaps still dripping with baptismal water, Paul laid hands on them and "the Holy Spirit came on them, and they began speaking with tongues and prophesying" (Acts 19:6).

Again, to quote Dr Martyn Lloyd-Jones:

> *If your doctrine of the Holy Spirit does not include this idea of the Holy Spirit falling upon people, it is seriously, grievously defective. This, it seems to me, has been the trouble especially during the present century, indeed almost for a hundred years. The whole notion of the Holy Spirit falling upon people has been discountenanced and discouraged... surely one of the prime explanations of the present state of the Christian Church.*

(**Dr Martyn Lloyd-Jones,** *Joy Unspeakable***, Kingsway, 1984**)

THE VARIOUS THEORIES AND THE BIBLICAL ACCOUNT

Do we automatically receive everything at conversion? Certainly Cornelius' story indicates that an individual can be saved and filled with the Spirit on the same day. But for Paul and those in Samaria and Ephesus the case was very different. They heard the gospel and believed it, but they received the Spirit later through the laying on of hands. Clearly the teaching that we are automatically baptized or sealed by the Spirit at conversion is not borne out by these examples in the book of Acts. It wasn't Paul's experience.

Coupled with the notion that we receive everything at conversion is the idea that being filled with the Spirit is something that happens gradually. If you ask someone who holds this view, "Have you been filled with the Holy Spirit?" he will usually reply, "As I walk with God and grow in grace, I am steadily being more and more filled with the Holy Spirit." This may sound good but when Paul asked the Ephesian disciples if they had received the Holy Spirit, they were quite clear that they had not had this experience. But if Paul had asked them the same question after he had laid hands on them, they would have responded with a very definite "Yes!" – not a hope that this might gradually happen in due course.

In the New Testament, people were not vaguely aware of the Spirit. Either they had received Him or they had not. When the Spirit came upon them they knew all about it and so did everyone else present. Simon the Sorcerer saw something happen that so fascinated him that he wanted to buy the ability to give the Spirit (Acts 8:18).

A LATER EXPERIENCE OF SANCTIFICATION?

Nowhere do we find the apostles saying how good it is that some have believed in Christ as Saviour and been baptized, "But later, as you grow in your faith, you will need to make Jesus your Lord and then you will receive the fullness of the Spirit."

Peter and Paul did not tell new converts, "Now you must wait until you have a more mature grasp of your salvation before you ask for the Holy Spirit." Not at all! Immediately new believers were baptized, the apostles laid hands on them and expected them to receive the Spirit – which they did! The youngest believer, once he was saved, was fully qualified to receive the Holy Spirit.

THE "RELEASE OF THE SPIRIT"

When Peter and John arrived in Samaria, they did not tell the newly baptized believers that since they had become Christians through Philip's evangelistic ministry they simply had to allow the Spirit to be released from within them. Scripture plainly declares that the Holy Spirit "had not yet fallen upon any of them" (Acts 8:16). Only when Peter and John laid hands on them did they receive the Spirit.

What about the need of the original Twelve (and, indeed, the 120) to wait in the Upper Room until the Spirit fell upon them? Some have modelled their whole understanding of the receiving of the Spirit on what took place on the Day of Pentecost, and would encourage people to wait or "tarry" for the Spirit's coming – some have even "tarried" for many years, hoping that one day they might receive. But the record of Scripture shows that after the Day of Pentecost no one was ever told to "wait for the Holy Spirit". The youngest of believers simply received the laying on of hands. After Paul had baptized the men in Ephesus, he laid hands on them and they were instantly filled with the Holy Spirit.

I remember an occasion when a young woman called Celia was converted at one of our Sunday morning meetings. At the conclusion she asked me, "Is there not more than this?" She sensed the vibrant presence of the Holy Spirit in the meeting and did not want to miss anything in her experience as a young Christian. I invited her to my home on the following Saturday. She arrived eager to experience the Holy Spirit for herself.

She brought a friend with her who had been so impressed with the transformation in her life over the previous week that she also wanted to become a Christian. I had the joy of leading this friend to the Lord straight away.

After this, Celia reminded me that she had come to learn about receiving the Holy Spirit. I took some time to open the Scriptures and explain to her the basis of her expecting to receive the Spirit, and as a young Christian six days old in the Lord she immediately asked if I would pray for her. Her friend, who was by now about twenty minutes old as a Christian, immediately asked if she too could receive the Holy Spirit in the terms that I had explained.

I replied that of course she could and had the joy of laying hands upon both of them and praying for both of them, whereupon the Holy Spirit came upon both of them and they began to sing in tongues to the Lord Jesus with all their hearts. One was a Christian of six days; the other was a Christian of twenty minutes. "For the promise is for you and your children and for all who are far off, as many as the Lord our God will call to Himself" (Acts 2:39).

CHAPTER 4

EMPOWERED BY THE SPIRIT AND THE WORD

For me, being baptized with the Holy Spirit was like the knocking over of a first domino in a line of dominoes which are still falling. The implications for my church life were radical.

At the time of the early outbreak of charismatic life there were two schools of thought. One was that this was a private and personal experience which need not interfere in any way with your normal experience of church-going. The other was a realization that something fresh and new was happening that demanded a new wineskin to cope with the new wine.

Jesus warned about the dangers of pouring new wine into an old wineskin and said that no one used new cloth to sew up an old garment. The presence of the Holy Spirit was fresh, exciting and attractive. Jesus was so much more manifestly present amongst us. Surely we were not meant to interpret this experience in purely private ways. The Scripture says that the manifestation of the Spirit is for the common good (1 Corinthians 12:7). Evidently, if others were to benefit, there had to be a sharing of the gifts in a public context, not exclusively in private.

The gathered church is meant to be a place where the presence of the Holy Spirit is evident; you can't miss Him if He is manifest! We are expected to be a Spirit-filled community, "speaking to one another in psalms and hymns and spiritual songs, singing and making melody" to the Lord with all our heart (Ephesians 5:19). As Gordon Fee argues, "Perhaps most noteworthy from the available evidence is the free, spontaneous nature of worship in Paul's churches, apparently orchestrated by the Spirit himself. Worship is expressed in a variety of ways and with the (potential) participation of everyone (1 Corinthians 14:26)" (Gordon Fee, *Paul, the Spirit and the People of God*, Hodder & Stoughton, 1997).

THINGS MUST CHANGE

Structures had to change. Space had to be made for God to freely work amongst us. Gradually it became clear that the widespread growth of charismatic life was resulting in fresh expressions of church. People who had no previous experience of this kind of church began to gather in homes and informal contexts to worship and celebrate the presence of the Holy Spirit.

Those "heady" days seem long ago now. Many of the house churches which I helped to get started have grown to a substantial size. Several that began with one or two dozen people are now in their several hundreds, and what for many began as "the house church movement" seems to be rapidly becoming the "warehouse church movement" as worshippers crowd into premises formerly used for industrial purposes but now packed with enthusiastic worshippers of God.

Lessons learned in the informality of private homes had to be translated into a new setting. Relaxed intimacy could continue but the developing of relationships had to be pursued in multiplied small groups.

Worship inevitably became affected by the new setting and the growing numbers. Musical instruments, PA, platforms and overheads all had to be brought into use. Nevertheless, the manifest presence of the Holy Spirit is non-negotiable. Paul defines the true people of God as those who "worship in the Spirit of God and glory in Christ Jesus and put no confidence in the flesh" (Philippians 3:3).

Paul describes church life as awash with the Holy Spirit. In Corinth he urged that things should be done decently and in order so that, for instance, there should only be two or three prophesying, and two or three speaking in tongues and being interpreted. The New Testament church was profoundly aware of the presence of God. Even outsiders would be undone and uncovered, "declaring that God is certainly among you" (1 Corinthians 14:25).

Sadly, this had not been my previous experience as a member of a good evangelical church which was greatly enriched by the outstanding preaching ministry of its pastor. I had often been arrested, convicted, comforted and inspired by his superb preaching gift, but during the hymn-singing that preceded his teaching one never encountered the manifestation of the Holy Spirit.

Clear biblical factors rooted in the presence of the Holy Spirit were missing in our church life. There was need for restoration in the church, not merely personal renewal or even revival but structural restoration. Foundational issues had to be addressed. Things had to change!

Following years in Bible College, I found myself invited to become the pastor of a Free Evangelical Church, and as I set my course for major change I was drawn to such scriptures as Ezra and Nehemiah and the prophets who endorsed, encouraged and exhorted those men and their companions.

RESTORING ZION

I notice that Israel, which had formerly celebrated the presence of God not only on their wilderness journey, but also particularly in the Jerusalem Temple, had been finally exiled through their disobedience. Ezra and Nehemiah represented restoration figures. They wanted to see the city of God rebuilt and the house of God restored. They were prepared to make the long and costly journey to re-establish Zion.

Nehemiah was heartbroken when he heard that Jerusalem's walls were down and its gates burned. Anybody could walk in and out. All distinctiveness was gone. It was open country. The glory of Zion, as described in David's psalms, was lost. Nehemiah burned with passion to rebuild the city. He and Ezra longed to see the Temple freshly established. Urged on by Haggai and Zechariah, they went about their task with the promise from God that the glory of this latter house would far surpass the glory of the former.

Such scriptures profoundly affected me. I wanted to see not simply a personal enjoyment of the gifts of the Holy Spirit. I wanted to see a glorious church. I wanted to see the city of God reborn.

Of course, Nehemiah and Ezra and their fellow countrymen were not simply facing the problem of architecture and a physical building programme. The nation had been in exile in Babylon, away from God's presence. God had finally judged them, as the prophets had repeatedly warned them that He would.

Exile was the ultimate judgment. Just as Adam and Eve were banished from Eden, so Israel was ejected from the Promised Land of blessing and God's presence. Psalm 137 tells us that by the waters of Babylon they sat down and wept when they remembered Zion. Their captors mocked them, inviting them to entertain them with some of Zion's favourite songs. But they mourned, "How can we sing the Lord's song in a foreign land?" (Psalm 137:1–4).

As we began to welcome the presence of the Holy Spirit, and one by one a congregation of believers became filled with the Holy Spirit, our church life was transformed. Our worship became full of God's presence and virtually unrecognizable compared with what we had previously experienced. The presence of the Holy Spirit changed everything, not only in the life of each individual but in our corporate experience. As we more and more felt the presence of God, we began to understand that we were fully accepted sons by grace.

Later, a rediscovery of the doctrines of grace underlined our acceptance and set us completely free. We could wholeheartedly identify with Psalm 126:1: "When the Lord brought back the captive ones of Zion, we were like those who dream. Then our mouth was filled with laughter and our tongue with joyful shouting." Yes, we found that we could laugh and shout in the house of God. We were coming out of a kind of exile back into the presence of God, and discovering that for freedom Christ had set us free in His wonderful presence.

THE GOSPEL IN WORD AND POWER

Paul described his apostolic ministry as bringing about "the obedience of the Gentiles" (Romans 15:18). Nations locked in disobedience would be confronted with his call to return to God and to be "obedient from the heart to that form of teaching" which he brought (Romans 6:17). Paul was incredibly effective in his task. He impacted great cities steeped in pagan cultures and established strong, outgoing churches. For example, the Thessalonians turned "from idols to serve a living and true God" (1 Thessalonians 1:9) as a result of his ministry. How did he enjoy such incredible success? When Paul wrote to the Thessalonians, he commended them for their faith and reminded them that his gospel had come to them not in word only, but in power and in the Holy Spirit (1 Thessalonians 1:5).

To bring about the obedience of faith among modern heathen cultures, we need the same crucial ingredients in our message. Paul's method was not only "words". Words alone can be totally ineffective. As Eliza Doolittle cried out in total frustration, "Words, words, words. I'm so sick of words… Show me!" Modern people might well have the same problem with a gospel that is "word only". And yet I must point out that words are crucial. How can obedient faith be established without a message being heard? In days of increased spiritual experience and manifestations of power, we must not turn our backs on the role of biblical doctrine.

The gospel comes in word. It is good news that has to be understood. You don't just catch Christianity like catching influenza; nor do you simply attend exciting meetings, hoping simply to get caught up in the euphoria. Philip's first question to the Ethiopian was not, "Do you feel it?" but, "Do you understand?" Jesus said that the unfruitful pathway in his parable represented those who did not understand the word. The Thessalonians, in contrast, received the word "not as the word of men, but for what it really is, the word of God" (1 Thessalonians 2:13). They understood it, believed it, respected it and found that it "performs its work in you who believe" (1 Thessalonians 2:13).

So fundamental was the spread of the word in the New Testament church, that Luke described the growth of the church in these terms: "*The word of God* kept on spreading" (Acts 6:7); "*The word of the Lord* continued to grow and to be multiplied" (Acts 12:24); "*So the word of the Lord* was growing mightily and prevailing" (Acts 19:20) (all italics mine). Luke could have said that the churches multiplied, or the number of disciples grew, but on these occasions he spoke about the ever-increasing impact of the word of God. The whole world has been lied to and it is the church's responsibility to bring the truth to it.

The apostles regarded preaching as crucial. They filled Jerusalem with their doctrine. When forbidden to speak any more, they pleaded for boldness to open their mouths. When blessed with numerical success and the growing practical problems associated with that success, they insisted that others looked after practical matters. They were determined to give themselves to the word of God. Even after His resurrection, fully equipped with a body that could appear and disappear at will, Jesus did not overwhelm His disciples with supernatural tricks, but, opening the Scriptures, "explained to them the things concerning Himself" (Luke 24:27). This was consistent with His earlier ministry, during which "He saw a large crowd, and He felt compassion for them because they were like sheep without a shepherd; and He began to teach them many things" (Mark 6:34).

RELIGIOUS HUNCHES

We can never jettison this emphasis, especially today when people are so full of their own ideas about God and life. Even when showing interest in the Christian message, many want to continue to eat of the tree of independent knowledge of good and evil instead of submitting their minds to what God has revealed in his word. J. I. Packer has said: "People have got into the way of following private religious hunches rather than learning about God from his word" (J. I. Packer, *Knowing God*, Hodder & Stoughton, 1973). Human perspectives of God and His requirements fall far short of God's revelation. "You thought that I was just like you," God complains in Psalm 50:21. A. W. Pink said: "The foundation of all true knowledge of God must be a clear mental apprehension of his perfections as revealed in Holy Scripture. An unknown God can neither be trusted, served, nor worshipped" (A. W. Pink, *The Attributes of God*, Baker Book House, 1975).

People not only come into the church with their own views of God, but sadly, many within the church develop their own concepts by simply gathering up crumbs that fall from the wrong tables. So we hear such things as, "I don't think of God like that" or "My Jesus would never say that."

Sadly, some Christians have developed such a love and respect for the word itself that simply to hear it faithfully expounded can become an end in itself. Delighting in "sitting under" good teaching, we can be in danger of becoming like Ezekiel's hearers – that is, those who love to hear a love song sung well, or an instrument played well (Ezekiel 33:32). The fact is that Paul's gospel was with word and power. He reminded the Corinthians, "my message and my preaching were not in persuasive words of wisdom, but in demonstration of the Spirit and of power, so that your faith would not rest on the wisdom of men, but on the power of God" (1 Corinthians 2:4–5). After Paul's ministry, supernatural power flooded the Corinthian church, and as B. B. Warfield has argued:

> *There is no reason to believe that the infant congregation at Corinth was singular in this. The apostle does not write as if he were describing a marvellous state of affairs peculiar to that church… We are justified in considering it characteristic of the apostolic churches that such miraculous gifts should be displayed in them. The exception would not be a church with, but a church without such gifts… Everywhere the apostolic church was marked out as itself a gift from God by showing forth the possession of the Spirit in appropriate works of the Spirit – miracles of healing, miracles of power, miracles of knowledge whether in form of prophecy or the discerning of spirits, miracles of speech, whether of the gift of tongues or of their interpretation. The apostolic church was characteristically a miracle-working church.*
>
> **(B. B Warfield, *Counterfeit Miracles*, Banner of Truth, 1972, pp. 4–5)**

Or as F. F. Bruce argues:

> *The testimony of the New Testament writings to the regularity with which these phenomena accompanied the preaching and receiving of the gospel in the early apostolic age is impressive in its range. The "mighty works and wonders and signs" which marked the ministry of Jesus (Acts 2:22) continued to mark the ministry of the apostles from Pentecost onwards (Acts 2:43)... Similarly the recipients of Peter's first epistle are reminded how the gospel was first preached to them in the power of "the Holy Spirit sent forth from heaven" (1 Pet. 1:12).*
>
> (F. F. Bruce, "Hebrews", *The New International Commentary of the New Testament*, Eerdmans, 1990)

Evidently the early church advanced through the preaching of the revealed word of God *and* through evidence of power in their midst. The advance of God's rule has always been through demonstrations of power. When Moses came out from Egypt leading the redeemed Israelites, power was demonstrated in signs and wonders and the opening of the Red Sea. When Canaan was inhabited, Jericho fell through the power of God, and other victories were won through the intervention of a God who acts. David advanced and he established his kingdom through God's powerful activity. As in the Old Testament, so in the New Testament the early church expected manifestations of God in order that the gospel might advance effectively.

Gordon Fee has argued: "The message of the gospel is truth accompanied by experienced reality... God verified its truthfulness by a display of his own power through the ministry of the Holy Spirit" (Gordon Fee, *God's Empowering Presence*, Hendrickson, 1994).

TRUTH AND FIRE

It has been a source of great sadness to me to see two schools of thought within the evangelical church over many decades now. Those who come glorying in manifestations of power sometimes seem dismissive of those whom they regard as "cold theologians". I once heard a man speaking at a large conference saying that theology was the enemy of the church and that if only we could abandon doctrinal perspectives, the church would be a happier place. What tragic nonsense!

We also see and hear those who love theological insight and savour the doctrines of Scripture expressing equally dismissive remarks about Christians who are enjoying God's power, as though they were mere children preoccupied with experience. How I long for a recovery of true biblical Christianity, where the apostle Paul, who wrote the book of Romans, also raised the dead! It seems that profound theology and great signs and wonders happily cohabited in Paul's life and ministry.

Jack Deere says, "No text of Scripture says that the Bible was given to replace the need for the miraculous confirmation of the gospel message." He adds, "The miraculous phenomena were not simply signs of the Kingdom of God, they were an essential part of it. Miracles and the Kingdom of God are inseparably linked" (Jack Deere, *Surprised by the Power of the Spirit*, Kingsway, 1994).

Many cultures less sophisticated than ours in the West seem to have no difficulty in embracing the supernatural dimensions of the gospel. The amazing evangelistic success currently taking place in China, for example, is characterized by such signs and wonders.

If we are to see a massive turning among the heathen so that they repent of their sin and reject their independence and embrace a life of the obedience of faith, we will need to see the same power and be submitted to the same apostolic doctrine as the apostle Paul brought to the nations so successfully. As a result of his clear declarations, he was able to establish churches of great clarity and authority, like that at Thessalonica, from which the gospel sounded out to the whole region with powerful effects.

CHAPTER 5

HEALINGS AND MIRACLES, SIGNS AND WONDERS

The Old Testament revelation of God shows him to be one who heals sick people. His very name "I am the Lord, who heals you" (Exodus 15:26 NIV) leaves that in no doubt. The psalmist reminds us not to forget his benefits and adds not only "who pardons all your iniquities" but also "who heals all your diseases" (Psalm 103:3). He healed in direct response to the prayers of Abraham, Elijah and Elisha, and also healed all who looked at the bronze serpent Moses lifted up in the wilderness (Numbers 21:9). He also kept their bodies, clothes and sandals intact for the forty-year journey.

When Jesus came declaring the arrival of the kingdom, He proclaimed that His powerful signs were the kingdom in action, a proof that the promised and long-awaited kingdom had manifestly come. The King had arrived and, with Him, the promised kingdom was at hand. It could be touched and embraced.

The kingdom carries with it the mystery of the "now" but also the "not yet". Yes, the kingdom has been inaugurated, but it has not yet been consummated. Strange contrasts can be found even in the ministry of the Lord Jesus. At one time we read that the power of the Lord was present for Him to heal (Luke 5:15) and at another, "He could do no miracle" because of their unbelief (Mark 6:5). When the kingdom finally comes in all its glory, Christ will make all things new and without exception the redeemed will receive their new, glorified bodies. Meanwhile, in this passing age, our experience will not be so uniform. If Jesus' ability to heal encountered some limitations in His own home town, we should not be surprised to encounter similar disappointments when aiming to see the sick healed.

A casual glance at the gospels reveals Jesus as one full of compassion and power, and spending much of His time in healing the sick. It has been said, with only slight exaggeration, that every time we meet Jesus in the gospels, He is either healing someone or just returning from healing or just going to heal. He turned no one away and it is sometimes recorded, "he healed them all" (Matthew 12:15). Matthew chapters 8 and 9, for instance, contain nine acts of healing or exorcism.

Jesus often initiated the healing rather than waiting to be asked and He responded even when a man confessed to partial unbelief. His tentative, "I believe; help my unbelief" was not rejected as inadequate. His disciples tried to withstand the demands of blind Bartimaeus, but Jesus was once again completely accessible and ready to heal.

A crowd of thousands followed Him one day as He climbed a hill (Matthew 15:29–38). We are told that throughout three days He healed all that were sick among them. Imagine the joy and the thanksgiving to God as not one person among the thousands remained sick. A hilltop filled with praising people with everyone healed! It must have been like a foretaste of the new earth when all will be finally healed and the kingdom will be fully expressed.

ANOINTED TO PROCLAIM FREEDOM

Jesus introduced Himself in Luke 4 as the fulfilment of Isaiah's promise. The Spirit of the Lord was upon Him and He came to release the captives and bring sight to the blind. He demonstrated a militant and urgent attitude when, for instance, He healed the cripple woman with His confrontational tone, "should not this woman, a daughter of Abraham, whom Satan has kept bound for eighteen long years, be set free on the Sabbath day from what bound her?" (Luke 13:16 NIV). For Jesus this was not a matter for debate – action was required; freedom was at hand.

Peter summed up Jesus' ministry in Acts 10:38: "God anointed Jesus of Nazareth with the Holy Spirit and power… he went around doing good and healing all who were under the power of the devil, because God was with him" (NIV). God empowered Him for conflict! He often seemed to regard sickness as an enemy. He was hostile to it. Was this a passing or fleeting attitude which Jesus adopted during His brief earthly ministry, or should we not see Jesus as the revelation of the Father, perfectly demonstrating His will and purpose? In fact, Jesus claimed that the Father, dwelling in Him, did His works (John 14:10). The gospels seem to reveal that God is essentially for healing and against sickness. If Jesus, who was God perfectly manifest in the flesh, adopted such a stance and spent so much of His time busily healing, why would we suppose that God the Father or the Son have now changed their attitude? Was Jesus perfectly representing the Father, or did He become distracted with secondary issues?

FAITH AFFIRMED

Jesus enthusiastically congratulated those who demonstrated faith in Him. The frail woman, apparently hidden in the crowd, was happy to remain unseen and unknown, but Jesus found her and affirmed her: "your faith has made you well" (Matthew 9:22). He celebrated the opportunity to make public the faith that she had when she secretly touched His garment. He showed the same enthusiasm when He marvelled at the centurion's faith when he invited Jesus simply to "say the word" and not come to his home. Saddened that He had not seen such faith in Israel, Jesus expressed real appreciation for the fact that the Gentiles were beginning to put their trust in Him. This, sadly, was in stark contrast to the unbelief manifested in His own home town, which left him amazed.

Faith clearly plays its part in the release of healing. I have often watched faith grow in a context where people are being healed. One

Sunday morning, having seen several healings, I approached one woman to ask what her problem was and she replied, "I have back pain, but I won't have it in a moment" – and she was right! When I prayed for her she was immediately healed. Another testified, "It's OK. I've just been healed while were you praying for the others."

Again, in a context where several were being healed, I recently was told by a woman that her pain was related to her spine being curved. I was immediately reminded of a doctor I had prayed for with a curved spine who had been completely healed. To my surprise, I heard myself saying, "It won't be like that for long!" and told her spine to straighten out. She began to shake quite violently and actually fell to the ground, but when she got up her spine was straight. She was thoroughly healed and had no more pain. Faith had suddenly welled up in my heart and I found courage to speak out.

COMPASSION MOTIVATES

Repeatedly Jesus' heart of compassion is seen as the motivational trigger that releases His power (e.g. Matthew 14:14 – He saw a great multitude and felt compassion for them and healed their sick). When Jesus healed the sick, God's mercy was perfectly demonstrated. Though others recoiled from one suffering with leprosy, Jesus, "Moved with compassion… stretched out His hand and touched him" (Mark 1:41). The power to heal was present and compassion moved Him into action. Men and women were given a demonstration of God's awesome grace and mercy.

When I was personally healed in answer to prayer, and the pain with which I had lived for years left my body, I was moved to tears, not simply by the loss of pain but by the awareness of God's amazing kindness. I knew of people far more seriously ill than I, but now God had personally shown me His mercy, His compassion. He set me free and I was overwhelmed with His kindness.

I often see people weep when they are healed. His personal touch and tenderness become manifest in their lives. God's presence draws very near.

FULL SALVATION

The salvation that Jesus brought was many-faceted. The Greek word *sozo* itself presents the translators with a challenge. Sometimes it is translated "saved", and other times "healed" (Matthew 9:22). He clearly came to make people whole in the fullest sense. The man lowered through the roof by his caring, believing friends received forgiveness of sins and healing for his body. Jesus as a Saviour saved people from many things such as guilt, judgment, stormy lakes, hunger, shame, humiliation, embarrassment at a wedding party, and bondage to a lust for money. When Zacchaeus received Jesus into his house and his attitude to possessions was transformed, Jesus proclaimed, "Salvation has come to this house." Salvation is a very broad theme which clearly includes His healing power.

SIGNS ARE POINTERS

Jesus appealed to His signs and wonders as confirmation of His authenticity. If people struggled with His phenomenal claims, let the healings speak!

Later, Paul would make similar claims that his gospel was not in word only but also in power and in the Holy Spirit (1 Thessalonians 1:5; see also 1 Corinthians 2:4). The writer to the Hebrews reflected on how the gospel that was brought to them was not only in speech, "God also testifying with them, both by signs and wonders and by various miracles and by gifts of the Holy Spirit according to His own will" (Hebrews 2:4).

WHAT WAS PREACHED?

Some would argue that the apostles did not preach healing as such, but what kind of message was Paul preaching when we are told that a certain man, lame from birth, was listening to the apostle? Paul, seeing that he had faith to be made well, commanded him to stand (see Acts 14:9–10). What had Paul said that led the man to receive faith to be made whole? Surely he must have been preaching a Christ who heals, not only one who forgives sin. Paul preached Christ; the Christ of the gospels, the one that Peter also proclaimed at Cornelius' home in Acts 10:38, whom God anointed with the Holy Spirit and power and who went about doing good and healing all who were oppressed by the devil.

What did Paul preach in Galatians? Later he wrote to them, asking what prompted the miracles that took place there (Galatians 3:2). Did they experience miracles through keeping the law or "by hearing with faith"? What did they hear with faith? Surely they heard about the Jesus of the gospels and the kingdom that he had inaugurated, which included the probability of miracles. From Paul's preaching they heard words that inspired faith for miracles.

WHAT DID JESUS PROMISE?

Jesus promised, "Truly, truly, I say to you, he who believes in Me, the works that I do, he will do also; and greater works than these he will do; because I go to the Father" (John 14:12). Because He is now exalted at the right hand of the Father with all authority, He can continue to fulfil these great works through His church. Jesus stated it plainly.

The apostles were not alone in performing signs. Stephen and Philip, who were called to fulfil a role of caring for the poor widows, performed signs in Jesus' name. We are told that Philip was "preaching the good news about the kingdom of God and the name of Jesus Christ". This was followed by "signs and great miracles taking place" (Acts 8:12–13). Stephen, full of grace and power, was performing great wonders and signs among the people (Acts 6:7). The ministry which Jesus began continued through His followers.

MODERN SCEPTICISM

Sadly, healing is often regarded with scepticism in the modern church in the West, resulting in a lack of confidence even among those who embrace the Bible's promises as authentic for today. In spite of the vulnerability and lack of faith produced by this mindset, ever-increasing numbers of healings are taking place in our ranks.

In the last few years I have personally witnessed people being healed from shingles, arthritis, celiac disease, back, shoulder, head and leg pain. I have seen damaged arms immediately healed and no longer needing the support of a sling, people's spines straighten, the power of ME broken, and a woman in a wheelchair, bound for twenty-one years, stand up and walk completely whole. One unsaved woman on her first visit to our church sat weeping. The lady sitting next to her asked what her problem was and encouraged her to ask an elder to pray for her, which I happily did. Later, X-rays showed that her formerly damaged kidney was now perfectly whole. Her pain disappeared. A few weeks later, she was converted, was baptized and joined the church.

Such stories are multiplying. Some in our ranks are increasingly taking to the streets and offering to pray for the sick with growing success. The pastor of "The King's Arms", a *Newfrontiers* church in Bedford, recently told me that their teams had seen over 200 people healed on the streets.

Yes, there are often mysteries and deep disappointments. Not all are healed in our experience. We have much to learn but feel we have started a journey and there is no point in turning back.

Having prayed for one lady with ME and receiving a letter from her a few weeks later to say that she could hardly believe that she was now fine, doing the school run, pushing her trolley around the supermarket and perfectly whole, I found myself a few weeks later praying for another with the same sickness. Having prayed for her, I moved on to the next person and then heard her crying. She had felt no improvement. Everything within me wanted to say how sorry I was. In the pit of my stomach I was challenged, "Shall I continue to pray for others?" But then I learned of a man I prayed for who every day used to have to come downstairs backwards because of his severe pain. Now, after prayer, he was running downstairs completely pain-free. Another lady said she put her own shoes on herself that morning for the first time for twenty-one years. An embarrassed student at university shyly told me that she had not wet the bed again since we had prayed some months earlier at the end of a meeting. Another pastor I had prayed for sent me a photo of his recently born son after he and his wife were told they were not able to conceive.

A medical doctor sent me photos of her spine before and after praying and showing the healing that had taken place. Stories are multiplying and almost every week I see people being healed.

Throughout churches with which we work, and especially in a context of evangelistic outreach, we are experiencing an increasing number of healings and miracles. Undoubtedly we have so much more to learn and often feel like amateurs.

Taking such a journey also leads to pain, disappointment, frustration and mystery. You come face to face with the fact that so many people suffer daily, carry huge burdens into their daily life, agonize over sick relatives, and yearn to be made well.

It's probably easier to leave the whole subject alone, and not put oneself in a context of pressure, anguish, embarrassment and vulnerability, but, on the other hand, Jesus said, "Truly, truly, I say to you, he who believes in Me, the works that I do, he will do also; and greater works than these he will do; because I go to the Father" (John 14:12). So by God's grace I think I will aim to carry on.

Chapter 6

TRANSFORMING GRACE

Recovering church life to New Testament norms is not simply a matter of charismatic gifts and new church structures. The people of God must be restored to a fresh appreciation of all that is theirs in Christ. Freedom from law and condemnation opens the door for praise and wholehearted dedication to God.

Sadly, many a Christian is more aware of a sense of failure and condemnation than of reigning and rejoicing. If we are going to see the church restored, we must first see individuals breaking out of the legalism that often pervades the atmosphere of evangelicalism.

"Amazing Grace" is more than the title of a grand old hymn that has been given a facelift and even reached the pop charts. For many of us, once steeped in the "do's and don'ts" of evangelical tradition, it has become a glorious, liberating secret. We have at last heard the unqualified statement of our absolute freedom from law which is the very heart of the gospel. The temptation to reduce our Christian experience to the mere observance of external regulations has yielded to the authority of God's word. "For under the Law I 'died' and I am dead to the Law's demands so that I may live for God" (Galatians 2:19, J. B. Phillips).

A DIFFERENT GOSPEL

Nothing has hindered the growth of the kingdom more than the ugly face of legalism. The devil realizes that undermining the very character of the gospel is far more effective than opposing it blatantly because he then reduces it to the level of an irrelevant religion. A piety consisting of "Don't handle, don't taste, don't touch!" may have the appearance of wisdom in self-made religion (the NASB margin says: "delight in religiousness"), but Paul tells the Colossians it is of no value against fleshly indulgence (Colossians 2:21–23). It is at least comforting to know that Paul faced the same kind of problem in the first century. He was amazed that his followers had so quickly deserted "Him who called you by the grace of Christ, for a different gospel; which is really not another; only there are some who… want to distort the gospel of Christ" (Galatians 1:6–7). John Stott has said: "You cannot touch the gospel and leave the church untouched, because the church is created and lives by the gospel" (John Stott, *The Message of Galatians*, The Bible Speaks Today, IVP, 1986).

Having told the Romans that they are freely justified and declared righteous as a gift "apart from the law", Paul replies to the obvious question that such a statement raises – namely, "What about the law, then?" In Romans 7 Paul explains that at one time we were married to the law. He is a hard, unrelenting husband. We were totally under his authority and he constantly points out our errors and shortcomings. Not only does he show us our faults and remind us of his standards, he never lifts a finger to help us. He is impotent to help. One further thing about this overbearing husband is that he is always right. What a husband! We are married to him for life and there is, according to Romans 7, no freedom to marry another since this would be a form of adultery.

Just to quench any last glimmer of hope on the horizon, Jesus quite plainly taught that the law would never pass away (Matthew 5:17–20). We seem to be permanently trapped into a marriage with a fault-finding, overbearing, meticulously correct husband who cannot actually help us and who also prevents us from marrying a new husband. Condemnation looms large.

THE WAY OUT

Is there no escape? Having painted the blackest possible picture, Paul goes on to show us the way out. The law will never die but –

glorious truth! – we were made to die to the law through the body of Christ, that we might be joined to another, to Him who is raised from the dead (Romans 7:4).

God reckons that those who are in Christ have died with Him, and the law cannot touch a dead man. We have been released or discharged from the law so that we can serve in newness of the Spirit and not in oldness of the letter. Laws cannot produce life; they only draw lines of right and wrong. Paul argues that if a law had been given that was able to impart life, then righteousness would indeed have been based on the law (Galatians 3:21), but the law is an impotent husband. He cannot impart life.

Now we have died to the law so that we might be married to a new husband, Christ, and bear fruit for God (Romans 7:4). Jesus is full of life. He is no impotent husband. He wants me to abide in Him and He in me, and I shall bear much fruit. A completely different arrangement! He removes my condemnation by actually removing my guilt and then He imparts life through our love relationship so that I can actually bear fruit for God. The tragedy comes when the new convert, having discovered free grace through the gospel, returns to the old husband of law in order to live out his new life. This always leads to bondage and despair. After a period of heaviness of soul, he comes back to Jesus to receive free pardon again and shake off his guilt. But all too often he fails to understand what he is doing and again imposes new laws on himself in order never to fail Jesus again. What a tangle! No wonder many Christians testify to being "up and down". I suggest they are more "husband to husband".

DISCHARGED!

We are discharged from the law. Imagine a soldier who had enlisted in Her Majesty's Forces for an agreed period. During this time he is subjected to all the rigours and discipline of military training. He is under authority. Orders must be obeyed meticulously. But the day comes when his agreed term is completed. He is discharged. On that very day he strolls carelessly across the parade ground – a free man. Suddenly, the sergeant major turns the corner and sees him.

Horrified at the sight of this slovenly soldier, he orders him to return, head up, shoulders back, and stand before him at attention.

At first the ex-soldier cringes at the familiar cry, but then remembers he is discharged. "Cheerio, sarge," he waves. Let the sergeant-major become ever so red in the face, let the veins stand out ever so prominently on his neck, it's of no consequence. He cannot command the discharged soldier any more!

We are discharged from the law.

It is essential for us constantly to recognize our death to law. It is no longer the basis for our relationship with God and never will be. We are married to Christ and our fulfilment as Christians is bound up in our love relationship with him.

All evangelicals know that they can never be justified by the law, but what they often fail to realize is that they cannot be sanctified by it either. The law always condemns. Its purpose is to bring us to Christ (Galatians 3:24). The tragedy for many believers is that they get caught in a trap. They reach a crisis when they feel deeply challenged by a word from God concerning their sanctification and they deplore their recent history. With new-found zeal they determine to do better in the future. But at that very moment they make the fatal error that will lead them to certain failure and distress. At the time when they most need to break the snare, they choose the wrong course. They begin to impose certain laws upon themselves in order to help them reign in life. They perhaps adjust their alarm clock for half an hour earlier. They determine to read the whole Bible in the coming year, and so on. These steps may have real worth in and of themselves, but they do not provide us with the keys to "reign in life". The mistake is in thinking that in order to reign in life we must do something, while the New Testament does not teach that. It says that we reign in life by receiving the abundance of grace and the free gift of righteousness (Romans 5:17).

NO CONDEMNATION

The problem for many Christians is that they always feel condemned. But the answer to condemnation is never simply to improve our performance. It is to reckon on our position through grace. God has justified us freely as a gift. Condemnation is to do with guilt, not with feelings or improved performance. If we, through grace, are declared "not guilty" by God, then we cannot be condemned. Only the guilty man stands condemned. It is God who justifies, and if God has declared us "not guilty", Satan cannot take us to a higher court. There is none. There is no condemnation for us, not because we have been doing well lately, or because we have set ourselves a new standard, but because we are in Christ Jesus. He has carried our guilt on the cross. The more we come to enjoy that truth, the more we will know how to refuse Satan's constant barrage of accusations aimed at getting us down.

If Satan can get us off our ground in Christ Jesus and onto the ground of our effort, he knows he has us in his grip. We may succeed for a while with New Year resolutions but even before the chill winds of February, condemnation looms large all over again. The law always kills in the end.

Not only are we free from law, we are also accounted righteous as a gift. Paul tells us that Adam was a type of Christ (Romans 5:14). We often think of other Old Testament characters as types of Christ – such heroes as David and Moses help us to see aspects of Jesus the King, or Jesus the Shepherd – but how does Adam typify him?

IN ADAM OR IN CHRIST?

Adam is a type of Christ in that when he sinned he did so as head of the human race. He thus made us all sinners. We were "in Adam" and therefore blighted by his sin and guilt. No amount of human activity could make us righteous and get us out of Adam. Even our righteousness was as filthy rags. Countless acts of kindness clocked up nothing on our account. As Thomas Brooks said, "Till men have faith in Christ their best services are but glorious sins." While still in Adam we remain unrighteous and guilty. We can do nothing to be released.

When we are born again we enter a new family with Jesus at the head. Just as Adam's sin and shame were put on our account and all our endeavours at righteousness could not free us from guilt, so now all Jesus' righteousness is credited to us. We are accepted as righteous in Him. Our shortcomings do not disqualify us – we are not relegated to a middle ground somewhere between Jesus and Adam. We are either in Adam and therefore guilty sinners, or in Christ and therefore righteous. Jesus Christ is our righteousness and He is the same yesterday, today and for ever, whether we feel spiritually high or low. A real grasp of this truth frees God's people from a constant round of condemnation and heaviness.

We are in the Beloved (Ephesians 1:6). God has a dear Son who delights His heart and we are in Him. Isaac had a son in whom he delighted named Esau. One day, Isaac's other son "clothed himself" with Esau and drew near to his father. Isaac felt Esau's clothing and smelled his smell. He blessed Jacob "in Esau" (Genesis 27). Jacob hid in his big brother as a trick and received his father's blessing, but we have been placed in Christ by a loving Father, who now blesses us for Christ's sake with every spiritual blessing. He is not, like Isaac, alarmed to find us hiding there. He has placed us there and is pleased to bless us for Christ's sake.

Just as some early Christians under Jewish influence were tempted to be circumcised to make sure they were acceptable to God, many modern Christians develop external religious habits to try to be worthy of the grace that God wants to give them freely. This problem is not unique to English churches. The wife of an elder in a church in Washington DC told me she had listened ten times to my tape on the grace of God in order to find freedom from past legalism. In Cape Town a lady approached me at the end of a meeting where I had been handling a similar theme. "Is it really true?" she asked me, with tears pouring down her face. She then told me about her church background with its legalistic practices which had completely robbed her of the joy of her salvation. Many, therefore, find themselves taken up with the details of externalism, preoccupied with lists of places to which they should not go, clothes they should not wear, things they should not do.

This, in turn, tragically affects the gathering of the saints. Preoccupied with the rules and regulations, we find ourselves watching to see if others are keeping them properly and fail to discover one another as true friends. When I realize I am "accepted in the Beloved" I find myself free to receive you who are also accepted. Now we are free to relate on a new basis altogether. Relationships within churches that are seeking restoration have been greatly affected by this truth.

DANGEROUS DOCTRINE?

Isn't this a dangerous doctrine, to say that Christians are righteous without reference to the law? Aren't we in danger of running riot – or doing whatever we like and still regarding ourselves as righteous? Paul anticipates that bone of contention in Romans 6:1 when he asks, "Are we to continue in sin so that grace may increase?" His reply is unyielding: "May it never be!" He then goes on to show that we who have been placed in Christ have been united with Him in His death and burial and that, having thus died, we are freed from sin.

When Jesus was taken from the cross He was buried in the tomb, burial being the final act declaring death to be past. At conversion we are commanded to be baptized in the name of Jesus and there our burial takes place – not as an effort to kill the old man, but as a declaration that our old man has died together with Christ. We do not bury people in order to kill them, but bury them because they have died. We are not told to seek after a "death to sin" experience but to acknowledge that by virtue of being joined to Jesus we are partakers of His death (Romans 6:4; Colossians 2:12). In the New Testament this is as much a statement of fact as the declaration that two men were crucified with Christ, one on the right and the other on the left. We believe that two men were crucified with Christ. We must similarly receive the truth that we were crucified with him (Galatians 2:20).

I do not remember sinning in Adam in the Garden of Eden, nor do I remember dying on the cross with Christ. However, the Bible says that both have happened as a matter of fact (Romans 5:17–21). Now I am to live in the awareness of that fact.

IT'S TRUE, SO RECKON ON IT!

Paul goes on from the foundation of knowing it to be truth with the command that we should therefore reckon it to be true in our daily lives (Romans 6:11). We do not reckon it as true in order to make it true, but because it is true. I was helped in this matter when I once arrived at Barcelona airport to be told that the time was four o'clock in the afternoon. My own watch told me that it was actually three o'clock. As an Englishman I had now to pretend that the time was four o'clock when I knew perfectly well that it was actually three. Strangely, I did not find that I had to screw up my willpower to make myself believe that it was four o'clock. The truth of the matter was that when I was in Spain it was four. So it is with us as we step out of Adam into Christ. I do not have to reckon, concentrating my willpower to believe that I am now dead to sin. The Bible teaches that when you are in Christ you are dead to sin, just as when I was in Spain it was four o'clock. Therefore, reckon it to be so!

The gospel sets us free from sin. It is good news indeed. First, it delivers us from condemnation and makes us righteous as a gift. Then it releases us from the power of sin and makes us slaves of righteousness.

Having understood our clear ground of victory, the Christian life becomes a walk of faith. We fight the good fight of faith. When Abraham was promised that he would father a son, he could have strongly contested it. All his previous experience argued against that possibility, but instead he became fully convinced that what God had promised He was also able to perform (Romans 4:21). He grew strong in faith, giving glory to God. When the Scripture promises us freedom from sin we are prone immediately to consider our previous track record and we fail to listen to the life-giving word. Faith comes from hearing and hearing by the word of Christ. If God has promised it, He is able to perform it in us and through us and to write His laws on our hearts, thus freeing us from the power of temptation. The righteous man shall live by faith.

GOOD NEWS, NOT GOOD ADVICE

Any delay in a full realization of this promise in daily life does not negate the promise any more than the delay in Isaac's birth did. Either the promise is true or it is not. When Abraham fell short in his early experience it did not disqualify him from total fulfilment later. He was restored to the promise. So we too must learn to confess and receive forgiveness for failure but not abandon the goal of promised freedom. Many come to regard failure as inevitable and settle for constant confession as the Christian way. It is essential to let the word of faith work in us, telling us what the truth of the matter really is. We must go on believing until full realization is our experience. Although the Good News Bible translates Romans 6:14 as "sin must not rule over you", happily the gospel is even better news than that and actually says, "sin shall not be master over you" (see, for example, AV, RV, RSV, NASB, NIV), "for you are not under law but under grace".

CHAPTER 7

WORSHIP IN SPIRIT AND TRUTH

True worship must involve our whole being. Mind, heart and will must harmonize to magnify His name. We must praise Him with understanding, so we shall not encourage mindless ditties. Exhortations to "try to lift the roof off this time" have more to do with FA Cup finals than worship, and to be told to "sing it as though you really mean it" is sacrilege. What is the difference between that and an outright invitation to be hypocrites? If any worship leader feels he has to make such a request, then everyone has already missed the point of worshipping in truth. A careless mental attitude prevents true worship.

THANKS A LOT

Jesus wants us to express our appreciation. Thanksgiving is an appropriate attitude towards God. J. I. Packer says, "No religion anywhere has ever laid such stress on the need for thanksgiving, nor called on its adherents so incessantly and insistently to give God thanks as does the religion of the Bible" (J. I. Packer, *A Passion for Holiness*, Crossway Books, 1992).

Paul taught that man's rebellion against God began with failure to express thanks. "Although they knew God, they neither glorified him as God nor gave thanks to him" (Romans 1:21 NIV). Lack of gratitude characterizes the unbeliever who fails to acknowledge God and His standards of righteousness, as Paul goes on to say in Romans 1. Christians should stand in stark contrast, constantly expressing their thankfulness to God for who He is and what He's done. As we do this, our thanksgiving will be replaced by praise.

"Well played!" "Great shot!" "Wonderful meal!" "You look magnificent!" We praise others for many reasons and enjoy expressing approval – it's part of our emotional fulfilment. God wants us to praise Him continually. John Piper, in his outstanding book *Desiring God* (IVP, 1986), says that we tend to dislike people who crave praise or plaudits, wondering what's wrong with them. He says, "We admire people who are secure and composed enough that they don't need to shore up their weaknesses and compensate for their deficiencies by trying to get compliments." So why does God want our praise? Piper continues:

> *God is not weak and has no deficiencies. "All things are from him and through him and to him" (Romans 11:36). "He is not served by human hands as though he needed anything since he himself gives to all men life and breath and everything" (Acts 17:25). Everything that exists owes its existence to him and no-one can add anything to him which is not already flowing from him. Therefore God's zeal to seek his own glory and to be praised by men cannot be owing to his need to shore up some weakness or compensate for some deficiency.*

Piper argues that because God is unique and glorious it is appropriate for Him to draw our attention and seek our praise. For,

> *If God should turn away from himself as the source of infinite joy he would cease to be God. He would deny the infinite worth of his own glory… What could God give us to enjoy that would prove him most loving? There is only one possible answer, himself! If he withholds himself from our contemplation and our companionship, no matter what else he gives us he is not loving.*

Our praise is most heartfelt when our minds are engaged. When my wife and I were living in the USA, we endured American football on television. My untrained eye saw little to get excited about. Men crunched one another with bone-shaking tackles and kept stopping the action. Oh, for some flowing soccer! My American friends might wait eagerly for the Superbowl, but my praise was muted – most of the time I didn't know what was happening.

As time went by and I began to understand and appreciate the skills on display, I started to enthuse and praise what was praiseworthy. I understood that the bone-shaking tackles *were* the action and the skill of the quarterback to throw so accurately at a fast-moving target while under enormous pressure was amazing!

Many praise God in a limited way because they have never spent time getting to know Him or what He has done.

A true soccer fan is qualified to praise an excellent move which leads to a magnificent goal. His understanding of the skills involved heightens his enjoyment. But let's add another dimension – identification. A soccer fan can enjoy any goal, but what if it's his team that scores? What if his son is playing, if it's his son whose pirouettes leave the defence standing and slam the ball into the net? Now we are talking about ecstatic praise. What proud father could remain unmoved and offer some polite applause? When Mary was by the empty tomb, she didn't note with detachment that a resurrection had taken place; she was overwhelmed because her Jesus was alive again!

WE PRAISE WHAT WE ENJOY

Quoting C. S. Lewis, Piper says, "We delight to praise what we enjoy because the praise not merely expresses but completes the enjoyment. It is its appointed consummation. It is not out of compliment that lovers keep on telling one another how beautiful they are. The delight is incomplete until it is expressed." Piper adds, "There is the solution. We praise what we enjoy because the delight is incomplete until it is expressed in praise. If we were not allowed to speak of what we value and celebrate, what we love and praise what we admire, our joy would not be full" (John Piper, *Desiring God*, IVP,

1986, quoting C. S. Lewis, *Reflections on the Psalms*, Harcourt Brace & World, 1958, pp. 93–95).

Joyfully expressed praise is often followed by admiration and reflection. Outbursts like "Well done!" and "Fantastic!" give way to other sentiments, such as "Isn't he wonderful?" or "She's amazing!" I can imagine the women who sang "David has slain his ten thousands" reflecting afterwards, "Isn't he magnificent? I wish I knew him."

A time of worship is a fresh opportunity to get to know God. We can grow in faith as we declare glorious things about Him and to Him. Often there will be a breaking free from sin as we touch His holiness and experience His love melting our hearts afresh.

Truth sets us free, and truth sung with faith and in the power of the Holy Spirit can have a mighty liberating effect upon us.

Many praise God in a limited way because they have never spent time getting to know Him or what He has done. Their thinking has been man-centred rather than God-centred. "How can I be fulfilled, get my hurts healed, have a successful marriage?" Even our worship can be self-centred: "I like quiet, gentle songs." "I prefer up-tempo celebration praise."

Worshippers must be preoccupied with the object of their worship. Some people foolishly say, "I don't want to know more about God; I just want to know God more." But the more I know about a person, the more I can actually know that person. The more I know about His character and accomplishments, the more I'm qualified to praise Him. So let's expand our knowledge of God. After theology lectures at London Bible College I just wanted to sit and worship, or stand and shout praise.

GETTING TO KNOW GOD

We often say that God is all-knowing and present everywhere, but do we really think about that? God knows everything all the time. He never has to look in his filing system to find out the number of grains of sand or how many hairs there are on your head. He knows what Henry VIII was thinking when Anne Boleyn was beheaded.

The universe baffles our minds, but no star slipped into existence while He wasn't looking. He knows, names and numbers them all. And everything was made from nothing! We make things out of matter that already exists. We take paint that is made, brushes we can see and a canvas we can handle. God "conjured" the universe out of nothing. We're amazed when a conjurer pulls a rabbit out of a hat, but, as R. C. Sproul points out, God started without a rabbit or a hat. He brought the universe into existence out of nothing. That's creativity! (See R. C. Sproul, *The Holiness of God*, Tyndale House, 1985.)

God is all-powerful and all-good. Isn't that great? Praise God for His omnipotence! Wouldn't it be terrifying if He were very powerful, but not *totally* powerful? Wouldn't it be dreadful if He *almost* had control of the seasons, the tides and the orbits of suns and moons. Imagine living in a world where God was not quite sovereign. Alternatively, imagine His being totally sovereign but not consistently good. What torture it would be for the universe if God's morality were less than perfect, if He had cruel streaks to His nature, or if He didn't care about right and wrong! We'd feel very insecure if an angel leaked the news, "God's power will run down in twenty-five years because creating and sustaining the universe has taken so much out of Him!"

The reality is, He's eternal, omnipotent, omniscient, good, just, holy, righteous, loving and glorious. What a God we have! The God and Father of our Lord Jesus Christ. Of course we want to praise Him. The more we know, the more we appreciate. The more we meditate on Him, the more our heart sings for joy.

EMOTIONALISM?

Many have dismissed a joyful, liberated expression of worship as mere emotionalism, but C. H. Spurgeon said, "I would sooner risk the dangers of a tornado of religious excitement than see the air grow stagnant with a dead formality" (C. H. Spurgeon, *Autobiography*, Banner of Truth, 1962). Of course emotion will be released – God has commanded it! We are told to rejoice before

Him, clap our hands, shout and sing.

The meetings that our reserved, English, conservative culture has produced are far removed from the Jewish roots of our heritage. In the name of reverence, many have banned clapping or the raising of hands from their churches. These are replaced by the whispering associated with a library or museum: but true reverence has to do with obedience, and God has commanded us to worship Him wholeheartedly. Let's reverently obey Him!

We are told that David and all the house of Israel were celebrating before the Lord with all kinds of instruments as they brought the Ark to Jerusalem. Suddenly, God struck a man dead for touching the Ark. He was judged for his presumption. However, having replaced the Ark by the correct, God-appointed Ark-bearers, David did not walk sedately to express his reverence, but even *after* that fearful manifestation of God's holiness he danced before the Lord with all his might (2 Samuel 6).

Some have argued that Old Testament worship was external with its clapping, dancing and use of instruments, whereas New Testament worship is internal because it is in spirit and in truth. However, we have often been left with something that is neither spiritual nor truthful. The New Testament says, "you greatly rejoice with joy inexpressible and full of glory" (1 Peter 1:8). Many evangelicals are in danger of joining forces with liberals, selecting verses here and explaining away verses there. The liberal's assertion, "It doesn't really mean he multiplied the five loaves" is not so different from, "Of course it doesn't mean real, indescribable joy."

Some modern theologians teach that the wedding guests at Cana did not actually taste miraculously provided new wine. It's sad to see many a good man arguing for the reality of new wine in Cana, but failing to lead his congregation into the "new wine" that Jesus is providing today.

Tragically, traditions that bind rather than loose have developed in church life during the cold years of spiritual bondage. Established church services leave very little room for true delight in God. Any who claim that their genuine authority is the Bible, not church tradition, must by God's grace make adjustments to obey His word (Matthew 15:6).

It has even been suggested that God developed denominations with their different styles of worship in order that we could select the one that reflects our preference and suits our temperament. All extroverts can join the Pentecostals, while more sober believers can settle elsewhere. What a tragic misunderstanding of God's purpose.

God is seeking those who will worship Him "in spirit and in truth", not "in temperament and preference". In God's glorious kingdom extroverts will learn to be hushed in awe before Him and those formerly inhibited will be drunk with new wine. Peter did not argue on the Day of Pentecost, "These are not all drunk as you suppose but are a group of extroverts who prefer this kind of worship." Certainly there will be great diversity in times of worship, but the variety should not be a reflection of our human failings and limitations but an outshining of the glorious multicoloured grace of God.

The house of God should be the gate of heaven (Genesis 28:17). God wants His house rebuilt that He might take pleasure in it and appear in His glory.

The Holy Spirit wants to lead us into greater heights and depths of praise. The New Testament spiritual house made of living stones must outshine the Old Testament temple.

Paul argues that if the old covenant of death and condemnation was with glory, how much more will the new covenant of the Spirit and righteousness abound in glory (2 Corinthians 3:9–11). The bright moon may dominate the night sky, but it is barely visible by day when the sun's glory fills the heavens.

Prophetic songs accompanied by Spirit-gifted musicians were present in the Old Testament. The radical church must shake free from the shackles of timid and drab conservatism. In looking for our true biblical roots, we must joyfully unearth the atmosphere of the New Testament church.

A NEW TESTAMENT CHURCH
AT WORSHIP

As Dr Martyn Lloyd-Jones has put it in describing the New Testament church:

> *Here is a gathering of men and women who are filled with the Spirit of God, and each one of them has got something; one a psalm, one a doctrine, one a revelation, one an interpretation, one a tongue. When one gave his contribution the others rejoiced and they praised God together; and they were all in a state of great joy and glory and happiness.*
>
> *Our danger is that we tend to judge and to think of the New Testament meetings with what we are familiar with in our deadness. Here is joy, here is inspiration, here is illumination, here is something that is given by the power and the work of the Spirit. There is so much life and power that the Apostle has to say, "Now you have got to control this. Let everything be done decently and in order." There were excesses in the church at Corinth, but what does Paul say to them? Does he say, "Never speak in tongues again, never prophesy again, never give vent to these feelings that you have within you." He does not say anything of the sort. The whole atmosphere in the early church was charged with the Spirit and they expressed that in psalms and hymns and spiritual songs.*
>
> *The really important question for us to face is, are we like the early church, are we like the early Christians, rejoicing and praising God, filled with gladness and joy so that we amaze the world and make them think at times that we are filled with new wine? Let us avoid all excesses, let everything be done decently and in order, but above all quench not the Spirit. Rather be filled with the Spirit and give evidence of the fact that you are.*

(Dr Martyn Lloyd-Jones, *Westminster Record*, Vol. 43, No. 9)

It is the ultimate scandal that people ignore the church because she is so boring. Her meetings are so predictable and grey. God has made a world of magnificent colour and variety, but it is only a garment that will ultimately be discarded. Though they have such a fleeting existence, God does not make two snowflakes alike. But the glorious church will live for ever, a bride adorned for her husband. She is the pinnacle of God's creative skill, destined to show forth the multicoloured wisdom of God (see Ephesians 3:10). How she needs to arise, shine and put on her beautiful garments of praise, and worship in spirit and in truth.

As churches have grown in size and are now often gatherings of hundreds rather than scores, the kind of meeting described by the Scripture and referred to here by Dr Martyn Lloyd-Jones will inevitably be affected. Paul describes a setting where each one present has potentially got something to contribute. With hundreds present, that becomes impossible but every endeavour should be made in local church life to embrace the activity of the Holy Spirit and to make space for those who will contribute in the large meeting with all the diversity that prophetic utterances and the like contribute. Some of the characteristics of the meeting described above will be found in smaller house groups and occasional clusters of house groups. Also, church prayer meetings provide a context for more spontaneous worship where songs are selected intuitively by the individuals present in response to what has already happened in the meeting.

Larger meetings will almost inevitably have worship leaders who have a huge, frightening responsibility to stand before hundreds of people as they draw near to God and aim to determine their pace and direction. That's scary! That should get them on their knees praying for help! It's not just about which tune to use or "let's start with a fast one to wake them up". We are talking about something profound. They are helping the saints fulfil their reason for living, namely to worship God and encounter Him in life in His temple.

As they select the songs, they are determining the words that hundreds of people will have on their lips for an extended period of time in a meeting. They are directing the thoughts of a whole congregation. Songs, therefore, need to be selected with great wisdom and great dependence upon God.

I was absent when one of our church members, Stuart Townend, first introduced his song "In Christ Alone" in our church. People were raving about it. When I heard it on tape in my car, I couldn't hear all the words, so I wondered why everybody was so excited. But the next Sunday I was in the meeting and felt the impact of the magnificent truth contained in Stuart's powerful lyrics. We must not keep singing songs that have no content. Let's sing songs that absorb our minds and expand our understanding of God.

Having said that, we are ultimately not satisfied with objectivity but crave encounter. As John Piper says, "In the end the heart longs not for any of God's good gifts but for God Himself. To see Him and know Him and be in His presence is the soul's final feast. Beyond this there is no quest. Words fail. We call it pleasure, joy, delight but these are weak pointers to the unspeakable experience" (John Piper, *Desiring God*, IVP, 1986).

We must not worry that this kind of worship is not "seeker friendly". I have non-Christian friends who have come to our Sunday morning worship and said to me, "We just cried. What did we touch? What was that?" This question came from a successful businessman of many years' standing, a tough man of the world. When we worship we want the unsaved to feel the impact and know that God is there.

"IT'S A PITY THE CHURCH ISN'T LIKE THIS"

Once, when we hired a holiday camp for a teens' and twenties' week, the employees of the camp were amazed at the life and joy expressed in our praise and worship. "It's a pity the church isn't like this," they said. We were able to tell them of a number of churches that were very much like that! The unconverted could see the need for new wineskins to contain the life of these young people who were thrilled and filled with God.

Hundreds of non-Christians filled two adjoining halls – one being used for a disco, the other for a boxing match. The manager expressed his concern for us when he asked, "What about the noise?" We replied that *they* would have to put up with it! They not only put up with it but pressed their faces against the windows of our meeting hall to witness the life there.

On a spring bank holiday Sunday, about 400 praised God and sang and celebrated on Brighton seafront. They could be heard from quite a distance away. Many stopped to listen and take literature. On arriving a little late, I parked my car in a nearby street. A couple passed me wanting to discover what the joyful scene was about. "It sounds as though the pubs have turned out," they said.

It was not an enemy of the church who recorded that their first public meeting looked like a crowd of drunks! Dr Luke seems neither embarrassed nor ashamed of the seemingly insulting comparison. We are exhorted not to be drunk with wine but to be filled with the Spirit (Ephesians 5:18). There are real comparisons as well as contrasts between being full of the Holy Spirit and full of new wine, and the Bible draws that to our attention more than once.

Not only should we as individuals know the new wine of the Spirit, but our church life must be sufficiently flexible to cope with the joyful exuberance that such "drunkenness" brings. New wine in new wineskins. New songs from new creatures enjoying a new covenant. God deliver us from staleness at any point. He makes all things new.

CHAPTER 8

CONSIDER YOURSELF ONE OF THE FAMILY

When I was converted I lost all my friends. As teenagers we had grown up together. We enjoyed marvellous experiences and our friendship was very real. Late into the night we would talk about our innermost hopes and fears. It broke my heart when none of them wanted to come with me into my new-found Christian life. I often wept for them in prayer. After a while, I began to weep for myself. I was so lonely. It was wonderful to know my sins were forgiven and that I was going to heaven, but life was miserable in the here and now.

On Sundays I was inspired by the minister's wonderful preaching, but I was lost in the crowd and nobody seemed to notice me. Gradually, as time slipped by, I grew in experience and found that this was true for so many. Formal acquaintance seemed to be the standard in the church. People who had known one another for years were still on handshake and surname terms. Real friendship such as I had grown up with and so valued was almost entirely missing. After a couple of years I was received into membership and received "the right hand of fellowship". But nothing changed.

ATTENDING MEETINGS!

The Christian life, therefore, seemed to be a matter of losing all my old, ungodly friends and in their place simply attending meetings. In the agony of my loneliness I threw myself into every meeting available. My week included Sunday morning and evening; on Monday, a prayer meeting; on Tuesday, Young People's Fellowship; on Wednesday, Bible School; on Thursday, the male voice choir (I had to go somewhere!); on Friday, I was an officer in the Boys' Brigade; and on Saturday, there was a prayer meeting. But in all this – no friends!

When people began to meet in homes, sharing their new-found charismatic experience, they started finding natural friendship again. The very informality of the front room was so different from always meeting in the church building on its hard, upright pews or chairs.

Christian names replaced surnames and, unexpectedly, Russian-style hugs replaced handshakes. Intimate prayer fellowship where God's presence was felt also melted cold formality. Drunkenness through alcohol, which often released and apparently enriched my old friendships, was replaced by a new Holy Spirit informality which led to laughter, joy and freedom among Christians. New experiences drew us out of our shells – the first stumbling attempts at speaking in tongues and interpretation or prophecy, gathering around individuals in need to lay hands on them and pray. All these experiences helped to knit people in friendship.

For some, the leap to real friendship proves so difficult that something else creeps in. Instead of genuine friendship comes a strange super-spirituality: syrup-sweet choruses followed by obscure readings or visions, shared in an atmosphere of growing unreality.

A new experience of the Spirit opens the way to the possibility of friendship, but it does not guarantee it. We do not automatically make friends by meeting in charismatic prayer meetings instead of formal church services. True friendship calls for open-eyed confrontation as well as melting moments in worship.

TRANSPARENCY AND VULNERABILITY

True friendship has to be developed outside of Christian meetings. For friendship to flourish there must be openness, honesty and loyalty. We must be willing to come out from behind our masks and religious jargon and get to know each other openly.

But of course lasting, valuable friendships are not surface deep. They are frequently challenged by times of misunderstanding, thoughtlessness and plain sinfulness. How do we cope with the pressures? We try to work out a loyalty based on the commitment required of new covenant people. We are not casual friends; we are blood brothers and sisters in covenant with God and one another. I do not mean a secret, exclusive covenant, limited to a certain framework of elite believers. Jesus commands us to be committed to loving our enemies and opponents – he certainly expects us to love all our Christian brothers and sisters. John's first letter is full of exhortations to prove our faith by love for the brethren.

Local churches must become churches where true friendships are formed and a framework is built for their outworking. New converts called out of a way of life must find that they are called not simply to attend meetings – even charismatic ones. They are brought into a family; they are part of a living community.

EXTERNALISM KILLS FRIENDSHIP

If a congregation is still within the pressures of evangelical legalism and bondage to externalism, true friendship will hardly ever take place. The terrible temptation to put on a front, or to justify one's existence by outward form, quenches the flame of natural warmth and affection. Our attitude to meetings must be like Jesus' attitude to the Sabbath – meetings were made for man, not man for meetings (Mark 2:27). Every service must come under close scrutiny. Is it purposeful? Why do we have it? Is it bearing fruit? What happens as a result of it?

When dead meetings and religious observances become part of our church life, they militate against real friendship because they militate against reality itself. Upon entering the very church building some people seem to change into other people. Natural speech becomes inappropriate. Normal ways of greeting one another disappear. People start tiptoeing and whispering. Is it any wonder that we have difficulty with warm friendships?

This whole approach is based on a totally wrong doctrine of the church building as the house of God. Evangelical believers know that the church is the people, not the building. We are His house. Why, then, are we not totally consistent with our doctrine? Some seem to think that the building itself is holy, and even that one end of it is more holy than the other!

AT HOME TOGETHER

What a contrast we find in the New Testament, where disciples are reclining at the table with Jesus and even leaning on one another. What an atmosphere there must have been when that band of men were together. What laughter! What joy! What seriousness! What zeal! What excitement! What fun! What friendship!

I thank God for the red-hot zeal for Christ that I find in my friends, and I thank God for the riotous times of laughter we enjoy together as well as the days of prayer and fasting. God has called us to be friends. Jesus called His disciples "friends". Abraham was the friend of God and it is difficult to say anything more profound than that.

It is because we feel ourselves to be friends of God that we are freed to be friends with one another. When our relationship with God is based on law (Old Testament or evangelical) we find it very difficult to relax together. We are commanded to receive one another as Christ received us. When I know that God has received you and me just as we are, "warts and all", I can receive you similarly. Neither of us has to pretend. Because of our genuine friendship we can actually help one another in reality. We can honestly share our hopes and fears, failures and frustrations, and our prayers and longings.

We will only arrive at the maturity God has planned for us as we encourage, exhort and admonish one another. The New Testament is full of commandments telling us to do a variety of things for one another. We can only obey these commands and discover their power when we get close enough to handle the discomfort and pain of such encounters.

There is something very attractive about close friends who trust one another, enjoy one another's presence and really care sacrificially for one another's wellbeing. Loneliness holds little to attract us. We might occasionally crave some solitude, but eight discs, a favourite book and a luxury item would hardly suffice to lure most of us to a desert island for the rest of our lives. We like company. Real friendship is a beautiful thing, but like most beautiful things, it does not come cheaply. It is possible to be a Christian and yet be devoid of satisfying friendships.

When we send out unfriendly vibes we will attract few close companions. If we are critical and hostile, few will seek our company. If you try to build relationships with others by giving them a display of your cutting humour towards a third party, don't be surprised if few entrust their secrets to you.

Friendship flourishes with those who accept others warmly and affirm them. We want to escape our loneliness by finding people with whom we can share our most intimate hopes and fears. It is only as we "open up" our hearts that we find the true release that friendship can provide.

Have hours of Christian counselling come to replace the joys of good, honest friendship? If we do not rediscover the comforts of deep and open Christian friendship, I fear that counselling specialists will multiply and intimacy will be by appointment! People who are gifted in counselling and willing to give their hours sacrificially to help the needy members of our churches will be in danger of supplying an escape from loneliness, instead of providing the specialist insights that they are peculiarly gifted to offer to the most needy.

If mutual acceptance opens the door to friendship, loyalty under pressure provides the means for keeping it open. If I share my secrets with you, I want to know I can trust you. I also want to know that you will be faithful to me even if I let you down. This requires enormous discipline in a world of disloyalty and in a context where Satan, the most disloyal creature in the universe, is committed to destroying everything beautiful. He hates covenant love and is aiming to make it scarce on planet earth!

How often friendships are lost because we fail to remember Satan's active hostility. How he loves to sow the seeds of doubt and distrust! He knows his only hope is to divide and conquer. If we remain loyal and true to one another, his hands are tied.

Loyalty means that I will stick with you even when I know your faults. Uncovering your hidden weakness will not make me forsake our friendship but will simply provide more motivation to pray and talk openly. True friendship has no time for "no-go areas". We must be free to talk about anything, yet not force the pace too quickly. Some have been deeply hurt by previous experiences and find it difficult to open up again. Nothing should be taken for granted as we progress towards full openness and transparency in our friendships. We need time together where there is opportunity to unwind and develop beyond the superficial.

In reality, Christians have a capacity for friendship which goes way beyond others' because we have a high and yet compassionate view of mankind. We know that people are worth it! Many of our contemporaries doubt that. Some see human beings as merely advanced animals, simply responding to various stimuli. Jean-Paul Sartre regarded humanity as "trash". Others experience sudden painful failure in their companions and are shocked and disillusioned by the sin factor, so that they give up on people.

Christians are uniquely clear about the nature of humankind. We know before we start on a friendship that this person will probably occasionally let us down. We understand this. We know that even Christians have their treasure in clay pots, and although we often contact the treasure we sometimes come up against the clay pot! Christians should be somewhat unshockable and therefore able to sustain friendship. We know about the apostle Peter's denial and King David's adultery. We understand flesh and blood.

We also understand grace and redemption and realize that we are being changed from glory to glory. Loyalty can be maintained even through painful failure. With God's help, bitterness and resentment can be overcome and discarded. We can always find grace to start again in a way that the unredeemed know nothing about.

Christians are also in a unique place to display friendship between the sexes. Free from male chauvinism, they can love, honour and respect friends of the opposite sex with great joy and fulfilment. Modern society, with its preoccupation with either sexual immorality or sexist rivalry, has made it very difficult for men and women to develop good, healthy friendships between the sexes that are free from undercurrents. Christians should be able to relax into excellent friendships with the opposite sex. Jesus loved not only Lazarus but also Mary and Martha. We can be free to love our brothers and sisters with equal joy and purity.

It is so easy to use people and drop people, to be offended by people and then prove disloyal at their time of need. Proverbs says, "A friend loves at all times" (Proverbs 17:17). Let's make sure that we make and keep friends well.

FRIENDLY WOUNDS

When I am assured of my brother's love and genuine friendship, I can receive correction that would be wounding from a comparative stranger. I can even come out of my shell and begin to do some admonishing myself when I know my relationship is secure. We would do well to study all the "one another" verses in the New Testament and ask ourselves how many of them are being obeyed in our local congregation and in our individual lives.

Confrontation can be very difficult, and many avoid it. But what wasted time could be redeemed in our lives if faithful friends started telling us some home truths about ourselves. It is only a good friend who will bother to tell you that you always dominate conversations, that you never listen to anyone else, that you are inconsiderate to your wife, that you are too soft on your children, that you put people off because your breath smells or you don't use deodorant.

Is this the kingdom of God, you may ask? Is it down to such pathetic details? Yes. It is the stuff of life. It pleases God when we learn to live securely in good relationships with one another and when frightened, lonely people are helped to find true friends and can start enjoying life instead of hiding behind outward forms. People who have been freed from loneliness and introspection make good friends of others – even of the unconverted. Yes – they become natural evangelists.

Large congregations do not provide the setting for close and intimate friendship to thrive. The small house groups which we have been led to make use of are far more helpful to that end.

SMALL GROUPS ARE INDISPENSABLE

As John Stott argued in his very helpful book, *One People*:

> *There is a need for large congregations to be divided into smaller groups such as one imagines the house churches were in New Testament days. The value of the small group is that it can become a community of related persons and in it the benefit of personal relatedness cannot be missed, nor its challenge evaded.*
> (**John Stott, *One People*, Falcon Books, 1969**)

He points out that the bar flourishes not because most people are alcoholics but because God has put into the human heart the desire to know and be known and love and be loved, so that many seek a counterfeit fellowship at the price of a few beers. He goes on, "I do not think it is an exaggeration to say, therefore, that small groups, Christian family or fellowship groups are indispensable for our growth into spiritual maturity."

The house groups into which churches have been divided are not simply Bible study groups or prayer groups, though evenings may often be devoted to either of those vital exercises. Nor is their purpose to produce a miniature version of the large Sunday congregational meeting. Whole evenings have often been given to outdoor picnics, house decoration, evangelism or church cleaning.

The house group leader and his wife play key roles, providing not only a warm, hospitable atmosphere but also helping the elders in the ministry of discipling. They have the care of the group and, under the elders' supervision, they watch over the little flock in their charge. As they accumulate experience they can be given more responsibility for the people, and so men can begin to display their potential as possible future elders.

They are particularly asked to watch out for and encourage new, emerging leaders. Thus the pattern for growth develops. House group leaders are in constant contact with their elders in both regular training and fellowship gatherings and also individually. So the burden of responsibility for the leadership of the local church is broadened and more people are finding their place of service in the body of Christ.

JETHRO'S ADVICE

God originally spoke to me on this theme through the advice Jethro gave Moses in Exodus 18:21. I was, at that time, pastoring a growing church and preaching twice each Sunday and once mid-week regularly. Jethro's advice to Moses to choose men to share the load proved as revolutionary in my life as it did in Moses'. I chose some able and faithful men; able, or nothing is accomplished; faithful, or they divide the church and destroy the work!

We discover our place by accepting one another and serving one another in love, not by being preoccupied with a constant search to identify "our ministry". As we offer our service we are appreciated, thanked, encouraged and corrected and thereby trained. Gradually, we find our particular place. Correction is to be seen not as an outrageous and impertinent invasion into our personal life but as a natural part of family relationships. It should not be reserved for encounters of crisis proportions. Disciples are like apprentices: always looking for improvement and open to adjustment.

Paul says to the Roman church, "you yourselves are full of goodness, filled with all knowledge, and able also to admonish one another" (Romans 15:14). We all have blind spots and our Christian friends can see us change by plain speaking.

HAPPY FAMILIES

We encourage men to take a responsible attitude towards their families as head of the home and to raise their children sensitively "in the discipline and instruction of the Lord" (Ephesians 6:4).

Although Sunday Schools are found in our ranks, most would want to emphasize that they merely provide back-up to the parental responsibility of teaching. We have abandoned the idea of aiming our evangelism at the children of the unconverted in order eventually to win the adults. We would much rather reach responsible adults, believing they will bring their own children.

We have a strong conviction that Christian family life can speak volumes in our crumbling society to many whose families are in sad disarray. We have to recover a sense of parental involvement in a day when drop-out parents can be blamed for much of today's juvenile delinquency.

Views on child-raising vary enormously, but Christians are privileged to know God's view. The father, as head of the family, is responsible for the state of his household. He must, therefore, be aroused from the apathy associated with modern-day fathers in order to fulfil his God-given role.

This also involves the recovery of the biblical order of relationships between husband and wife, abandoned by modern society and, sadly, by many in the church.

When the Israelites entered Canaan, God had already given them wonderful laws and principles that would make them stand out as a testimony to the nations. The greatest danger they faced was that of disobeying the Lord by worshipping the gods of the land and imitating the local people's horrific practices, which included child sacrifices.

Today's gods of humanism and liberal thinking are worshipped by many at a terrible cost. Our neighbours may laugh at the standards of the Bible, but they are apparently willing to pay the price of their worship by sacrificing their marriages and producing insecure and troubled children. As Bible-believing Christians, we must be true to what God has shown us and demonstrate to the world how family life is really meant to be enjoyed.

People who get married expect to be living alone no longer. But Jesus showed how even people living under the same roof can be living alone. He said that unless a grain of wheat falls into the ground and dies, it remains alone. The only way to be freed from "living alone" is to die to your self-interest. In that sense, a wedding ceremony is also a burial service. Two former individuals die in order to become something else. Something new is being created. They become one flesh.

To enable that marriage partnership to function properly there is a God-given order. It is not a case of "anything goes". The Christian home should be an expression of God's kingdom, therefore it has divine order.

HUSBANDS AND WIVES

A loving and mutually respectful attitude between husband and wife is the key to good family life. When children see their father loving, protecting and honouring his wife and giving her her true place in the home, they will learn to respect her themselves.

When a wife shows true heart submission to her husband, honouring the dignity he has been given as God's appointed head of the house, she demonstrates the way of obedience which the children can follow.

The right relationship between men and women in the home overflows into our corporate church life. People have often observed a preponderance of men in our churches. We live in days when many men of the world have rejected the church as being for women and children. They are, therefore, often surprised by what they find in our ranks. Men are not only present but are obviously enjoying one another's company as friends and are involved in the life of the church.

When I introduced the concept of "open worship" in my first church, I was saddened by the immediate predominance of the ladies in prayer and praise. I had no desire to stop them, feeling that the Bible gave them freedom to pray or prophesy (1 Corinthians 11:5), but I longed for the men to be at least as voluble.

I wondered why the ladies were freer to take part. Were the men lazy? Fearful? Self-conscious? Or simply lacking in the kind of fellowship that the ladies often enjoyed during the daytime?

Certainly, many of the ladies knew each other more intimately and often had daytime prayer fellowship.

MEN'S MEETINGS

I decided to introduce an occasional men's evening. It was an unstructured time for fellowship, praise and prayer, and proved an extraordinary turning point in the church's life. The men began to be friends together and enjoyed amazing times of praise and prophecy as well as hilarious laughter and fun. The Sunday meetings were gradually influenced and male/female contributions became balanced.

Later, when I moved to Brighton, we again started a men's meeting. We used the same unstructured style with great success, forming intimate friendships and enjoying wonderful times in the presence of God.

One could easily be misunderstood in making this point, but the truth is that there is a certain "something" in getting men together who mean business for God. We have certainly noticed what a profound impact lively men's meetings have on those recently converted. Many have their previous concept of the church completely shattered in one evening. At the risk of sounding simplistic, we do encourage our men to be men!

The ladies are still very evident and fulfilled in our church life. They take part freely in worship meetings through prayer, prophecy, healing, tongues, interpretation, singing, Scripture-reading, testifying, baptizing, breaking bread, praying for the sick, and indeed everything except those things uniquely restricted to the elders. Behind the scenes they also play as vital a role in church life as the men.

Some Christians don't feel the need to commit themselves to any local body of believers. They see themselves simply as members of the body of Christ at large and do not give their allegiance to any local assembly, thereby totally failing to grasp the fundamental purpose of body life as expressed in the New Testament. Jack Hayford, in his book *The Church on the Way* (Zondervan, 1985), tells how a guest at his church signed the visitors' book and beside her name indicated her home church to be "the body of Christ". For its address, she added "worldwide". I guess her name appeared on no one's washing-up rota!

R. C. Sproul uncompromisingly states:

> *It is both foolish and wicked to suppose that we will make much progress in sanctification if we isolate ourselves from the visible church. Indeed it is commonplace to hear people declare that they don't need to unite with a church to be a Christian. They claim that their devotion is personal and private, not institutional or corporate. This is not the testimony of the great saints of history; it is the confession of fools.*
>
> (**R. C. Sproul,** *The Soul's Quest for God*, **Tyndale House, 1992**)

THEY DEVOTED THEMSELVES

A phrase frequently used in the New Testament to describe people's response to the gospel is that they "were added" to the church. They did not simply get right with God; they were added to the company of disciples who devoted themselves to the apostles' doctrine, fellowship, breaking of bread and prayer (Acts 2:42).

The early Christians were devoted to fellowship. They were constantly together and relinquished the right to individualism and selfishness by no longer regarding the things they possessed as their own. There was no coercion. People had glad and generous hearts. They expressed commitment to one another as a spontaneous outworking of their new life in Christ. Their dynamic encounter with God drew them together in an intimacy of fellowship which made their previous experience of synagogue attendance pale into insignificance. They had all been drinking of the same Spirit and were all captivated by the same Jesus. They wanted to work out their new life by a thoroughgoing expression of love and loyalty to one another.

Chapter 9

EMPOWERING THE POOR

God has always intended having a people of His own in whom He can take pleasure and among whom He can dwell. Alan Stibbs once said, "The chief end of God in creation of man was to have a people of whom He could say, 'I am theirs and they are mine.'"

Of course, God's goal represents more than the average man's view of church-going and attending "a place of worship". It speaks of a community whose centre of gravity is in God and whose common ground above all else is that they belong to Him.

Maybe the nearest that the world has ever seen was the glorious New Testament church described in Acts 2–4 where "they were together", not simply together for an hour on Sunday morning but knitted and built together, part of Jerusalem's society but somehow apart from it. No man dared join them, be associated with them, be among them carelessly. Again, we are not referring to a Sunday service, but a recognizable company of people whose lives were extraordinarily interrelated at a profound depth, so that great grace was on them all and no one regarded any of their possessions (i.e. the things that they could have rightly regarded as belonging exclusively to them) as their own, but as commonly available.

This extended beyond the cash in their pockets. It even included property surplus to their requirements, so that Barnabas sold land in order to put the proceeds in the common pot.

OLD TESTAMENT PRECEDENT

God's compassion for the poor is well documented throughout the Old Testament. The nation of Israel was given clear instruction to build into their culture a generosity factor, which should have resulted in the needs of the poor being met. Although Scripture makes it plain that hard work, with its accompanying rewards, is regarded as the norm for life, nevertheless the poor, for one reason or another, will always be with us and we have a God-given responsibility to care for them.

God spoke in the Old Testament through three main channels – the law (clear rules and instructions for building not only religious life but the whole of society), the prophets (immediately inspired utterances addressing the people in their present situation) and wisdom literature (nuggets of truth to live by encapsulated in such books as Proverbs). All three – law, prophets and wisdom literature – included clear, authoritative instruction regarding how the poor should receive compassionate priority.

Such priority is at the heart of God's character and his great work of redemption. Sadly, in their backslidden state, Israel as a nation often omitted to fulfil their responsibilities to the poor and earned scathing denunciation from such prophets as Amos and Isaiah for the way that their greedy property acquisition resulted in the grinding of the faces of the poor in the dust.

God's judgments on Israel often came as a direct result of their failure to obey Him in these crucial areas of national responsibility. Such failures, together with their adulterous lusting after other gods, even earned them the name "not My people" (Hosea 1:9). As Christopher Wright points out, "The primary ethical thrust of the Old Testament is, in fact, social." Without this dimension of holiness, Israel's worship would never be acceptable. He continues, "Failure to honour God in the material realm cannot be compensated for by religiosity in the spiritual realm" (Christopher Wright, *Deuteronomy*, NIBC, Hendrickson/Paternoster, 1996).

The coming of the gospel did not mark the end of God's interest in the poor but released it on a mammoth scale, no longer simply to Israel's poor, but to the poor and needy of the nations. When the good news of Jesus came to town, God's values of grace, kindness and compassion came with it. The birth of the church on the Day of Pentecost was swiftly followed by an explosion of lavish kindness shared among the saints.

Many Jews who embraced Jesus as their Messiah would have been immediately disinherited by those who rejected Jesus of Nazareth. The saved would have suddenly become, overnight, poor and even homeless. But great grace was on them all and no one regarded anything he possessed as his own but they shared their possessions. Some even sold land and property and laid the proceeds at the apostles' feet for distribution among the poor.

Pentecost gave birth to an immediate Holy Spirit-inspired jubilee of caring and sharing. Such were the proportions of this huge welfare work that the apostles were in danger of becoming overwhelmed by it, so they appointed excellent men full of the Holy Spirit and faith who could handle such vital work. It is important for us to see that this was not the apostles' way of washing their hands of an unimportant and secondary preoccupation, but rather the outworking of their responsible attitude to ensure that it was very well handled as a priority in the emerging kingdom of God.

Pure religion is described by James in terms that we can often forget in our passion to extend the kingdom and win the lost. His definition is simple and clear-cut, namely: "Religion that God our Father accepts as pure and faultless is this: to look after orphans and widows in their distress and to keep oneself from being polluted by the world" (James 1:27 NIV). The gospel, put simply, is good news to the poor. James adds, "What good is it, my brothers, if a man claims to have faith but has no deeds? Can such faith save him? Suppose a brother or sister is without clothes and daily food. If one of you says to him, 'Go, I wish you well; keep warm and well fed,' but does nothing about his physical needs, what good is it?" (James 2:14–16 NIV).

SALVATION HAS COME!

Jesus taught more about handling money than any other single subject, declaring that it was impossible to serve God and money. When Zacchaeus said that he would give half his money to the poor and repay those he had cheated, Jesus did not merely say that he had made a noble decision. He said, "Today salvation has come to this house" (Luke 19:9). Zacchaeus, formerly dominated by greed, was now a free man. He had experienced salvation not simply in terms of going to heaven when he died, but in terms of an emancipated lifestyle. His bondage to money was broken.

It must be pointed out, however, that Jesus invited no one to embrace a life of asceticism and gave not the slightest hint that asceticism was inherently virtuous. His promise was that as we give, it will be given back to us "pressed down, shaken together, and running over" (Luke 6:38). Paul added that as we sow our seed, God will multiply it and increase our ability to give more (see 2 Corinthians 9:6–11). Poverty is, therefore, not to be seen as piety, and asceticism wins no points with God but rather holds the danger of leading us into a self-conscious endeavour to gain merit.

Jesus lived simply but was free to attend a wedding celebration and was even accused of being a glutton and a wine-bibber. He accepted material support from wealthy women (Luke 8:2–3) and he even scandalized some by accepting the extravagant anointing with extremely costly ointment, when according to the disciples' perspective, it would have been better used by selling it and distributing the proceeds to the poor (Matthew 26:9).

Though Jesus did not withdraw from the world, He made it clear that our investment and our confidence should not be in the passing pleasures of this world, where moth and rust can destroy. He encouraged His followers instead to lay up treasure in heaven. Paul advised Timothy similarly, telling him to instruct the rich in this present world not to fix their hope on the uncertainty of riches, but on God. They were to be rich in good works, to be generous and ready to share, storing up for themselves the treasure of a good foundation for the future (see 1 Timothy 6:17–19). It is said that when John D. Rockefeller died, his accountant was asked, "How much did Rockefeller leave?" His reply was classic: "He left it all!" Though it is impossible for us to "take it with us", Jesus gave us the alternative of sending it on ahead! He made it very clear that clinging tenaciously to money in this life is futile and short-sighted.

Poverty is a spiritual issue and clearly preoccupied the apostles, as demonstrated by Peter, James and John's words to Paul, urging him to remember the poor, something he was eager to do (Galatians 2:10). It is not to be regarded simply as the responsibility of aid agencies and governments. In the early church there was a clear connection between their care for the poor and dramatic growth. Today, the vast majority of people in the world are poor. If we are to change the expression of Christianity around the world, then we must remember the poor.

A GENEROSITY SPLURGE

The birth of the church was associated with an extraordinary splurge of generosity and freedom from possessiveness; being together seemed more important. Their needs became common: "If you need it and I've got it, I guess you should have it." Amazing!

This has not got much to do with giving 10 per cent to a weekly offering to uphold the minister and his needs and pay for the building not to fall down! This was radical common life. They were in fellowship, which did not mean they shared a cup of coffee after the meeting for a few minutes.

Koinonia is a fascinating Greek word. Among other things, it means "partnership". It's not strictly a religious word, but the church flooded it with fresh life and colour. Before they ever met Jesus, Peter, Andrew, James and John were in *koinonia*. They were partners in a fishing firm. They owned it together. If one was in problems with breaking nets, the others would rush to help. This was not a religious response, it was a partnership reality.

That partnership or common ownership lifestyle gripped the early believers. There were, of course, a lot of poor people among them. Devout Jewish parents probably disowned their recently converted sons and daughters. "If you follow Jesus of Nazareth, you are no longer my child! Forget inheritance. You are out! You are on your own!" Overnight many were disinherited. In the joy and wonder of Pentecost, the people clung together and helped one another along. They shared.

ASCETICS ANONYMOUS?

So, did nobody remain rich in the New Testament church? Was it an ascetic community made up of other-worldly, super-spiritual misfits abstaining from industry, commerce, profit and loss? It seems not!

Paul gave clear instructions to young Timothy as to how he should conduct his ministry. One thing he had to do was to "instruct those who are rich" (1 Timothy 6:17)… to leave the church? To get spiritual and poverty-stricken? Actually, no!

Timothy was to instruct the rich members of the church (GNB says "command them") firstly not to be conceited. Primarily it was to do with attitude. It's very easy for comparatively rich people to be conceited, self-sufficient and independent. They make their own plans, reach their own conclusions. They tend to stand apart from the crowd.

As James says, we tend to assume that "Today or tomorrow we will go to such and such a city, and spend a year there and engage in business and make a profit" (James 4:13). I don't suppose many in South Africa's townships, South America's shanty-towns or India's slums are overheard making the same claims. They are not wondering which university they will send their children to or which country they will visit for next year's holiday. Poor people don't have that kind of liberty.

James says the rich are in danger of thinking that they know more than they actually do. He brings the sharp reminder, "you do not know what your life will be like tomorrow. You are just a vapor that appears for a little while and then vanishes away. Instead, you ought to say, 'If the Lord wills, we will live and also do this or that'" (James 4:14–15).

The rich must beware of false security and pride. Fixing your hope on riches is a dangerous luxury, especially when the markets collapse. Timothy is instructed to remind the rich not to fix their hopes on uncertainty. "It's in the bank!" doesn't sound too good when the bank collapses.

READY TO SHARE

Instead Timothy must tell them "to do good, to be rich in good works, to be generous and ready to share" (1 Timothy 6:18). He is to remind them that this is only a "present" or "passing" world. There's another one coming. They need an eternal perspective. They are also to understand a strange mystery, namely, that somehow in being "rich in good works and generously sharing", they are accomplishing an extraordinary thing – they are storing up the treasure of a good foundation for the future.

Now there's a remarkable thing! Sharing with others is actually storing up for yourself. How enigmatic! Being generous to others is actually taking hold of what is life indeed (1 Timothy 6:19). Imagine! Giving and sharing sounds like losing out and having less for yourself. Paul says it's like storing up and planning wisely for the future. God has this extraordinary way of turning things upside down and challenging our worldview. He wants to set us free from the independence and isolation that money and possessions lure us into. He wants us dependent on Him and His wisdom and provision. He wants us to work this out in the context of a people, His beloved church, where kindness and generosity can be expressed and unity in Him demonstrated in tangible ways.

GET READY FOR POSSESSIONS!

One of the most dramatic ways in which God introduced this theme to His people was in the Old Testament when He was preparing them for their coming inheritance of the Promised Land. Owning land would be a new experience. Thus far as a nation they had known centuries of slavery, with its inherent poverty, followed by forty years of walking through the wilderness.

The forty-year journey was marked by the provision of daily manna, which had to be eaten on that day. No storing up allowed, except on Fridays! Owning, possessing and storing up were unknown. Now the Promised Land awaits with its new experiences of sowing, reaping, harvest, blessing, growth, reward for industry, or alternatively loss and poverty, whether through idleness or unavoidable tragedy, death or widowhood.

As we saw at the beginning, God primarily wanted a people, not individuals bent on personal success. So He established a principle that on the seventh year all debts were to be cancelled (see Deuteronomy 15). If on the sixth year your poor brother came to you for a loan, you were to freely give, not to ponder that on the seventh year you had to say goodbye to your loan. God wanted a generous, united people, not a divisive group of individuals fighting for their rights and developing a poor-and-rich divided society.

Similarly, if someone through his poverty had sold himself to you to become your slave, you had to free him on the seventh year, and "When you set him free, you shall not send him away empty-handed. You shall furnish him liberally from your flock and from your threshing floor and from your wine vat" (Deuteronomy 15:13–14).

With these instructions came the promise of God's blessing and prosperity. It required national faith. It required an awareness of their being a people together. It needed personal ambition and self-sufficiency to be put to death. They were going to dwell in God's land, like another Eden. God would be among them. They were to be a people together, needs being met, with the final promise that there would be no poor among them (Deuteronomy 15:4).

THEY FAILED THE POOR AND THE LORD

Tragically, God's ultimate fury with Israel was not rooted in their lack of religion but their failure to care for the poor. Prophet after prophet challenged them that they had failed to remember their calling. They had joined field to field, oppressed the poor and crushed the needy. While religiously fasting, they had failed to bring the homeless poor into their homes and failed to divide their bread with the hungry (Isaiah 58:7).

God's desire for a people sensitive to the needs of the poor and homeless was never embraced. Deuteronomy 15 was probably never worked out within Israel. In Acts 2 we see a spontaneous outbreak of Holy Spirit-inspired generosity which overwhelmed the young church.

Spontaneity can't be bottled or canned. The church had to live on after the phenomenal outbreak of Holy Spirit inspiration. It continued to multiply and spread. So Paul had to tell Timothy to remind the rich of their God-given purpose and privileges.

May God help us to stay sensitive to Him in His compassion to the poor, His tenderness towards their vulnerability and narrow choice range. Let's generously remember the poor, be a people together and store up the treasure of a good foundation for the future, truly taking hold of that which is life indeed.

CHAPTER 10

SHEPHERDS AFTER MY OWN HEART

Throughout my career as a church leader I have tended to emphasize the role of apostles and prophets. The church was originally built on the foundation of apostles and prophets (Ephesians 2:20), so they gave the people of God their fundamental identity. I have argued that we were not built on a pastoral foundation.

My argument has often been expressed by noting that pastors are called to care for and feed the flock and meet the flock's needs. An over-emphasis, therefore, on the pastoral role can result in preoccupation with needs. We could become need-centred instead of apostolic and prophetic, thereby missing God's intention and forgetting the bigger picture, building churches that gradually become foreign to the atmosphere of the New Testament.

I have been alarmed at the possible danger of a church becoming introverted, developing a culture where personal preference dominates and shepherds major on discerning and serving people's so-called "felt needs". However, in taking this stance, we may have failed to bring adequate positive biblical teaching about the vital role of pastors and teachers. They are, of course, the most visible ministers in the local church. They have the most "hands on" role among the flock.

CHANGING IMAGES

The danger of leaving a vacuum of biblical teaching is that other images can begin to emerge. Historically the role of the pastor has often reflected current trends. Prior to the Reformation, for instance, he was regarded as a priest – holy, separate, somewhat other and mystical in his celibacy, a mediator between the people and their God.

The Reformation shed fresh light on the unique mediatorial work of Christ and established the truth of the priesthood of all believers, who need no go-between but have personal, direct access to God through the work of Christ and the Spirit (Romans 5:1–2; Ephesians 2:18).

Post-Reformation and in the course of time, the Christian minister began to take his place in the developing culture and was often seen as a respected public figure in similar fashion to the local doctor or squire.

With the challenge of the Enlightenment, ministers began to feel a need for further academic qualification to prove their worth, and the comparatively modern "theological training college" was introduced. Intellect was trained in these specialist settings. The emergence of biblical criticism seemed to require further scholarship among pastors so that they could withstand the developing undermining trends of liberal scholars.

More recently, with the advent of psychology and therapy, the modern pastor has often felt the need to develop skills to discern the diverse stresses and strains of the members of his congregation, and he aims to gain insights into their temperamental strengths and weaknesses.

To bring us right up to date in our current consumer-driven society, pastors increasingly feel the need to develop management expertise, research and discern the market, project graphs, establish their five-year growth plans, and reflect the sophistication of a CEO.

If you are a pastoral elder, I wonder how you view your gift and calling?

BIBLICAL IMAGES

The most common biblical image for local church elders is a "shepherd", and though we feel fairly at home with the language of pastor or shepherd, most 21st-century urban dwellers have never actually met a shepherd nor are they likely to. The fact is that when God called Abraham, Moses and David they were all shepherds. They looked after sheep!

Jesus didn't say, "I am the good apostle" or "the good prophet", or even "the good evangelist", but happily claimed to be the Good Shepherd. Even our unsaved neighbours have a fondness for Psalm 23! Recently I was struck by the ongoing role of the shepherd revealed in the book of Revelation: "the Lamb in the center of the throne will be their shepherd, and will guide them to springs of the water of life" (Revelation 7:17). So shepherding continues into glory.

Indeed, the relationship between the shepherd and his flock gives us a fundamental revelation of the relationship between God and His people. God is revealed in Scripture as the ultimate Shepherd and Israel's journey through the wilderness provides the archetypal model of that relationship.

God was their Shepherd. His presence was essential. Without it they were unable to advance. His protection made them unique and unassailable. His provision met their every need in wilderness conditions every day through forty years. His guidance meant that they were being purposefully led to a Promised Land.

GOD'S UNDER-SHEPHERDS

Although the Lord was their ultimate Shepherd, men were enlisted to fulfil the shepherding role on His behalf. So Psalm 77:20 records, "You led Your people like a flock by the hand of Moses…" Moses was the extension of God's rule, the agent of His provision.

Later Moses is replaced by David, whom, we are told, God took from the sheepfolds from the care of the ewes and sucking lambs and brought to shepherd Jacob, His people. So he shepherded them according to the integrity of his heart and guided them with skilful hands (Psalm 78:52–53).

Moses fed the flock by giving them the law. David gave them the songs of Zion and through his inspired psalms fed them with phenomenal awareness and insight about God, His covenant commitment to them and the uniqueness of their relationship to Him. David emerged as the model shepherd king, prefiguring the great Shepherd King who would one day sit on David's throne.

One day a descendant of David would come as the perfect Shepherd King and rule God's kingdom in righteousness and peace. But we are told that the King won't rule alone; under-shepherds are also anticipated. Princes will rule justly, each providing shelter from the storm and streams of water in a dry country (see Isaiah 32:1–2).

"OTHER SHEEP I MUST BRING"

In the fullness of time the ultimate model Shepherd arrives, trains His disciples and sends them to make disciples of all the nations, teaching them to observe all that He has commanded them. As the apostles go, their intuitive strategy in obeying the great commission was to plant churches, establish flocks and appoint shepherds to care for them who would establish them in truth.

In the first century this implied bringing about a massive turnabout in people's thinking and lifestyles. Their worldview was in stark contrast to the gospel's Jewish roots. Embracing many gods or idols, they were notorious for their gross immorality.

The message could not consist of a simple "come back to God" call. Old Testament prophets had often pleaded with Israel to return to their God, but they worked from an accepted template of common history and the foundational place of the law. New Testament shepherds had no such common ground when encountering the Greek and Roman world. In the 21st century we now face similar challenges.

When Billy Graham came to the UK in the 1950s and '60s, the call to return to God would have been generally comprehended by that generation. Today we live in a different era and though people can be born again through encountering the simplest message, we must not assume that initial conversion will result in inevitable Christian maturity, or even basic understanding of Christian living.

The role of the modern shepherd includes a call to deconstruct people's previous worldview. Nothing can be taken for granted. Lives need to be re-formed. Coming from a fragmented and aimless society devoid of any trace of Christian values, people need to be re-socialized and taught how to relate in godly ways.

Raised on self-indulgence, consumerism and rampant individualism, the new convert won't automatically be transformed into a mature Christian who knows how to conduct himself in the household of God (1 Timothy 3:15).

God has promised to give His people shepherds after His own heart who will feed them with knowledge and understanding (Jeremiah 3:15). This feeding requires a radical approach. We are not called to build on a false foundation with teachings that imply merely personal fulfilment or the grasping of the individual's full potential, or how to love oneself. The shelves of many a Christian bookshop are filled with titles which appeal to personal fulfilment as the goal of the Christian life. Coming from a culture where demanding your personal rights seems to be the bottom line, new Christians hardly need that diet.

Shepherds after God's own heart will have a different goal. They understand the identity of God's flock and their aim will be to build a contrasting culture, an alternative community.

Paul thanks God that though his hearers were once slaves to sin, they "became obedient from the heart to that form of teaching to which [they] were committed" (Romans 6:17). His choice of words implies that they were now poured into a new mould and reshaped by truth.

Again, Paul speaks of a "standard of sound words" (2 Timothy 1:13). The word "sound" has a medical root and implies "healthy". We get our word "hygienic" from the original Greek word. False teaching, Paul says, spreads "like gangrene" (2 Timothy 2:17). We have been *entrusted* with a glorious gospel (1 Timothy 1:11) and must make sure that we are feeding the flock with authentic food and thereby proving trustworthy!

GRACE-BASED

In teaching the nations God's requirement, it is vital that we do not simply impose new rules and regulations but bring God's people to a new stance of grace and faith. This requires Spirit-inspired and empowered preaching and teaching that calls for and inspires a response in the hearers. Holy Spirit-inspired preaching brings about an encounter with God that demands a verdict and produces a changed life based on revelation, faith and love, not cold obedience to external rules.

God's flock will intuitively hear His voice and respond as truth is fed to them by called and anointed pastor/teachers. Gradually a culture of God-centredness will emerge characterized by worship, faith, grace, mercy, respect, service and the awareness of being an alien people whose fundamental citizenship lies elsewhere (Philippians 3:20).

SHEPHERDING LOVE AND CARE

The shepherd's ability to feed and be a channel of God's grace will result in the gathering of a flock. The sheep gather to the gifted anointing of shepherding and thus a flock forms.

The responsibility of the shepherds is not simply to expound truth but to develop relationships of love and trust, and in some cases to "parent" a flock often made up of those who have never been parented before. Paul says that he was among the Thessalonians like "a nursing mother" who "tenderly cares for her own children" (1 Thessalonians 2:7), adding that he also was "exhorting and encouraging and imploring each one of you as a father would his own children" (1 Thessalonians 2:11). Many in our modern world don't have true fathers. No one has helped to shape their lives. Many modern city-dwellers are lost and lonely, like sheep without a shepherd, distressed and harassed (Matthew 9:36).

There has never been a greater need for true shepherds to be raised up to care for God's flock, unafraid to use rod and staff when the need arises, and thereby keeping the flock safe and secure, at rest and able to lie down unafraid in green pastures.

A FINAL WORD

Paul, when speaking to the Ephesian elders, urged them not only to take heed to the flock and shepherd them, he also reminded them to "be on guard for yourselves" (Acts 20:28). If Jesus prayed, "For their sakes I sanctify Myself" (John 17:19), how much more must under-shepherds be on guard?

In John Piper's words, "Brothers, we are not professionals." Ultimately, we also are sheep. We need to stay very close to the great Shepherd, enjoying His smile, drinking in His lavish grace and being diligent to embrace His disciplines and training and follow His guidance.

Moses came from encounters with the Lord with a shining face. David made it his pre-eminent desire to spend days in the Lord's tent, feasting at His table and delighting in His presence. No under-shepherd is an end in himself, or has intrinsic superior wisdom. If Jesus said, "The words that I say to you I do not speak on My own initiative" (John 14:10), how much more must we be constantly receiving fresh grace and instruction.

God has promised "shepherds after His own heart". May we who are called to serve God's flock be the fulfilment of that promise.

CHAPTER 11

CHURCHES THAT PRAY

Jesus gave impressive priority to prayer, both as an example in His own life, and also in His teaching. His disciples, observing His personal prayer commitment and phenomenal success in life and ministry, asked Him to teach them to pray. They undoubtedly learned the lesson, so that in the book of Acts it is very evident that the early believers demonstrated their dependence on God in corporate prayer.

Forbidden to preach any more in Jesus' name, their reaction was not to panic or to plan but to pray. They reached beyond the authority of the hostile and powerful Sanhedrin to the One with total authority, the "Sovereign Lord". Our word "despot" is derived from the Greek word *despotes*, which they used. They knew where true authority lay and they knew how to access that power through believing and urgent intercession. As they prayed the place shook; they were again filled with the Holy Spirit and experienced fresh boldness while God continued to demonstrate His commitment to them through multiplied miracles.

Soon Peter was imprisoned and threatened with imminent execution. Again the church's immediate response was a spontaneous, fervent and effective prayer meeting. Angelic intervention led to Peter's release. The early church was undoubtedly a church that prayed. We would do well to emulate them. A praying church is a force to be reckoned with.

The apostle Paul constantly made reference to his own prayers for the churches and urged them in turn to pray for him and his apostolic ministry, expressing his serious dependence upon them. As Philip Hughes comments, "Prayer is stressed over and over again in the New Testament as a vital pre-requisite for the release and experience of God's power" (Philip Hughes, *Second Epistle to the Corinthians*, NICNT, Eerdmans, 1962).

Without prayer, local churches are telling God, "It's OK, we can handle things, thank you." The New Testament church suffered no such delusion. As the great Samuel Chadwick said, "It takes us long to learn that prayer is more important than organisation, more powerful than armies, more influential than wealth and mightier than all learning" (Samuel Chadwick, *The Path of Prayer*, Hodder & Stoughton, 1931).

LEARNING TO PRAY TOGETHER

But how do we pray together as churches? We need to acknowledge our dependence upon the Holy Spirit. The New Testament tells us that we don't know how to pray (Romans 8:26). We live in the overlap of the ages between the "now" and the "not yet". "Beloved, now we are children of God, and it has not appeared as yet what we will be" (1 John 3:2). The earth is still groaning, waiting for the fullness of the new age (Romans 8:20–21), and so are we. We are still awaiting our full redemption (Romans 8:23). In prayer we often become intensely aware of our limitations in this season. Into this context the Holy Spirit has been sent to help us in our weakness (Romans 8:26). We need to learn to pray in the Spirit together.

Believers gathering to pray need to begin by acknowledging the greatness of their God and their access to Him. It is not wise to begin a prayer meeting by completely focusing on the problem or challenges that we face. Like the early believers, we need a big view of God. Like Joshua before Jericho, we need to be more impressed and even overwhelmed by the majesty and omnipotence of the captain of the hosts of the Lord than by the height of Jericho's walls (Joshua 5:14). So before bringing our requests to God, it's good to honour and worship Him, giving the Holy Spirit opportunity to show us His greatness and our right to approach Him as confident sons of a loving Father.

Upon receiving fresh awareness of His power and our privileged relationship with Him, we can bring our believing prayers and intercession. This is part of what is meant by praying in the Spirit with His help and empowering.

Church members need to be encouraged to focus on the matter in hand, so we don't expect long prayers from any particular individual. We don't want anyone to take us on an inspired tour around the world's trouble spots! We need to know what is our immediate goal and then follow one another and agree with one another in prayer. So, if our subject is this weekend's evangelistic endeavour, we draw attention to that and stay with it. No one needs to be too lengthy and we remain with the theme until we have prayed it through. Sometimes we might raise our voices together as in Acts 4. Sometimes we break up into groups of two or three. Sometimes we endorse the prayers of individuals with our "amens", each of us entering into the other's prayers, not awaiting our turn to impress or experiencing frustration when someone else prays exactly what we were going to pray.

PRAYING WITH IMPORTUNITY

We stay with a theme because Jesus taught us to be importunate. He taught us to be like the friend at midnight who insisted on being heard or the woman with the unjust judge, who refused to be shaken off. This does not seem like praying to a heavenly Father. Surely God is not like that. But prayer that prevails must be like that. D. A. Carson comments: "many of us in our praying are like nasty little boys who ring front door bells and run away before anyone answers" (D. A. Carson, *A Call to Spiritual Reformation*, Baker, 1992).

As prayer follows inspired prayer, faith begins to grow. We experience the partnership of the Holy Spirit in prayer as a corporate body. He begins to stir our desires and our level of expectation. As the Puritans said, "We need to pray ourselves into prayer."

Undoubtedly some leaders are particularly gifted to lead the assembled group with prayer and faith. Their faith stimulates the faith of others and draws them out from passivity into true spiritual partnership in faith.

It goes without saying that we must be a people of true unity of heart to release power in prayer, not using self-conscious eloquence or imposing guilt on others because of our passion or despising the faltering words of those new to the experience of corporate prayer. If we are not careful, religious eloquence can replace childlike and genuine faith, while the newest convert can often bring a note of unvarnished reality that helps everyone back to earth and restores some authenticity.

To get a sense of direction for corporate prayer, elders must be open before God and they must be unafraid to lead. It is often through the lack of clear goals that prayer dissipates. Where relationships are well formed and love prevails, leadership is able to bring teaching and admonition to those who pray "off centre" prayers. Without instruction it is possible to fail to see issues through.

Into this context the gifts of the Holy Spirit are not toys but powerful weapons in the battle. Visions and prophecies often lead us in the conflict of prayer and give us a sense of direction.

We are not coming to the prayer meeting to do our duty or to demonstrate our religiousness. We have come to work. We did not choose Him, He chose us and appointed us, that whatever we ask the Father in His name, He will give us (see John 15:16). We are hand-picked askers.

"Why prayer is so indispensible we cannot say, but we had better recognise the fact even if we cannot explain it," wrote J. O. Fraser, the mighty pioneer missionary who worked so powerfully for God among the Lisu tribes of China in a previous century, resulting in the conversion of thousands. Fraser had a highly developed understanding of the power of prayer and he approached the matter very pragmatically when he said, "We often speak of intercessory work as being of vital importance. I want to prove that I believe this in actual fact by giving my first and best energies to it as God may lead. I feel like a businessman who perceives that a certain line of goods pays better than any other in his store and who purposes making it his chief investment" (Eileen Crossman, *Mountain Rain,* OMF Books, 1982).

PRAYER AND ACTION

It is a tragedy that anyone should regard prayer meetings as boring. When we look at the prayer meetings of the book of Acts, we always find them taking place against the background of action. The outbreak of the Spirit associated with the Day of Pentecost started with a prayer meeting. It is difficult to discern when the disciples stopped sitting in the house, in prayer, and began going into the streets with power. The next recorded prayer meeting is preceded by a brief visit to jail. It concludes with a shaking building filled with people who have had a fresh infilling of the Holy Spirit.

Because Peter was in prison again, the next prayer meeting happened spontaneously. It closed not with a formal benediction but by the release of Peter. A later prayer group in Antioch witnessed the call and commissioning of Paul and Barnabas to their apostolic work. Prayer meetings were continually alive with God's intervention. If our local church is inactive and merely carrying out a routine, the prayer meeting will soon reflect that in a lack of purpose and life. But if we are a people moving forward in God's purpose, our prayer times will be relevant and exciting.

Many contemporary churches would have stories to tell. For ourselves in Brighton, the conviction that we should buy a large centre that would seat nearly 1,000 people grew as the leaders were constantly praying about it. Finally we heard about a large industrial building placed on the market in the heart of Brighton. Although the church knew about our intention and had been praying for God's guidance, it would be true to say that a handful in our ranks were not thrilled with the thought of our spending a lot of money on a building. I was not at all unsympathetic to their perspective, since for years I had said that money should go into ministry, not into buildings. But God had clearly led us, so we pressed forward confidently.

The time came when financial commitment had to be expressed

by the people. I was teaching a series on Moses and the first Gift Day coincided with our studying Exodus 15 – Moses crossing the Red Sea. Strangely, the story seemed wonderfully appropriate. We were going to commit ourselves to a great step of faith that seemed way beyond our ability, yet we felt we had arrived there by simply obeying and following the Lord. Just like Moses at the Red Sea, we had to seek God's powerful intervention.

RESPONDING TO FAITH

In prayer we had asked that on the Gift Day we might raise £100,000 – a figure way above anything that we had raised before. In the prayer meeting on the previous Saturday morning I had felt a definite surge of faith. I believed that as we were praying God assured me in faith that we had already gained £100,000 and began to feel freedom to ask for more, maybe even approaching £200,000. I shared this with the prayer meeting and we prayed with fervour and faith.

We had a great Sunday. It was an extremely exciting day and we were going to cross our Red Sea. As I spent my final moments of preparation in my study at home, I was suddenly reminded of the great speech in Shakespeare's *Henry V*. I quickly grabbed my Shakespeare to make sure I was word perfect and concluded my sermon with some passion, with the quote: "and gentlemen in England, now abed, shall think themselves accursed that they were not here." It was a dramatic day! We concluded with the offering.

Later that night my wife and I were preparing for bed when I heard the letterbox clatter downstairs and what sounded like an envelope plop on to the mat. I rushed down and recognized the writing on it. It was undoubtedly the news we were waiting for. I took the envelope back upstairs, opened it carefully, unfolded the note and read the figures of the day's offering. It was fractionally short of £250,000. My knees buckled and I sat down involuntarily on the bed. We had done it! We had more than done it! I could hardly believe it. We had raised a quarter of a million pounds!

Subsequent battles concerning change of use of this industrial building to a place of worship, and battles regarding VAT were also fought in prayer and won.

I know countless stories of churches who can tell of God's wonderful faithfulness to them as they have pressed forward in faith and prayer. Churches have been planted, people have uprooted their families, moved house, found new schools and new jobs, sold property, bought property, gathered a nucleus and prayed a church into existence. Then they have gone on to battle in prayer for buildings and further church plants. So we go on co-labouring with God, constantly seeking His face and dependent on His activity with us.

Let me invite D. A. Carson to have the final word:

Much praying is not done because we do not plan to pray. We do not drift into spiritual life; we do not drift into disciplined prayer. We will not grow in prayer unless we plan to pray. That means we must self-consciously set aside time to do nothing but pray.

(**D. A. Carson, *A Call to Spiritual Reformation*, Baker, 1992**)

CHAPTER 12

A PROPHETIC
PEOPLE

I wonder what comes to your mind when you hear the phrase "a prophetic people"? Maybe you imagine a dishevelled line of individuals, clad in camel-hair garments and patiently waiting for their daily ration of locusts and wild honey!

Flowing beards and faraway looks seem to be fundamental to the role, so how can we modern sophisticates go to work from Monday to Friday in our cars and trains in collars and ties and be a prophetic people? How can housewives who take their children to the school gates sound a prophetic note?

OLD TESTAMENT ROOTS

First of all, we need to understand that the earliest prophets, like us, were actually people of their age. Abraham, for instance (the first person actually called a prophet in the Bible), was wealthy and lived in a sophisticated city. He had family and friends, flocks and servants. He was no mystic. Nevertheless, he heard from God and saw a vision which transformed and dominated his life.

He developed a relationship of amazing intimacy with Yahweh, and gained the title "the friend of God" (2 Chronicles 20:7). Before judging Sodom and Gomorrah, the question arose in heaven, "Shall I hide from Abraham what I am about to do…?" (Genesis 18:17). This led to a prolonged conversation between God and Abraham concerning that very judgment, thereby underlining the word of

Amos that "the Sovereign Lord does nothing without revealing his plan to his servants the prophets" (Amos 3:7 NIV).

Abraham was taken up with God's plans, not with his own sense of personal fulfilment. As he embraced these plans wholeheartedly, Abraham found his life's destiny and purpose. He was not on a "bless me" trip, even though God did bless him and made him a blessing to the nations. Without prophetic goals we tend to see God as existing simply to meet our needs. Even Abraham's spiritual development and growth in holiness were not essentially a personal and private matter. They were hammered out on the anvil of God's programme for the blessing of the world.

Following Abraham, the prophetic stream flowed on through Isaac, Jacob and particularly Joseph, whose whole life story reflected God's purpose for his people. Joseph saw visions, but these were no mere charismatic experiences. The rest of his life was a vindication and proof of their reality and relevance.

After Joseph, God raised up Moses, who is perhaps the Old Testament's most outstanding prophet. When he was a child his mother sowed the seeds of prophetic vision in his mind and heart. This meant that, although Egypt gave him education and wealth, he considered the reproach of association with God's prophetic people to be of far greater value. God's ultimate intention for his people mastered Moses and motivated his decisions. Later, a true prophetic call gripped his life so that "the Lord used a prophet to bring Israel up from Egypt, by a prophet he cared for him" (Hosea 12:13 NIV). The short-sighted and reluctant Israelites ultimately arrived at their destination through Moses' faithfulness to his prophetic call.

Next, the prophet Samuel introduced a new "kingdom age". The nation was familiar with prophets and priests, but they had never before been led by a king. Tragically, many subsequent priests and kings drifted away from God and even some of the prophets proved false. The true prophet was always in demand. Before the Israelites went into exile, the prophets called them to repent and return to God. In captivity Ezekiel outlined how the people should live. Jeremiah had informed them that they would return to the Promised Land, and to Daniel was given the privilege of seeing what would happen in the future. When the Israelites did begin to return to their land, Haggai and Zechariah encouraged them in the building programme. Jonah challenged their narrowness, and Jeremiah and Ezekiel raised their sights to a new promised covenant.

THE NEW DISPENSATION

Not only did John the Baptist prepare the way for Jesus, he also declared, "He will baptize you with the Holy Spirit and fire" (Luke 3:16). John was heralding a new day of the Spirit. Instead of being given only to individuals, the Spirit would soon be available to everyone.

What John the Baptist foretold, the apostle Peter confirmed. Taking the words of the prophet Joel, Peter applied them to the Day of Pentecost. "This is it!" he told the people who had gathered to see what was happening. "The new age has arrived! Sons, daughters, young and old will prophesy, see visions and dream dreams. The Holy Spirit is now being poured out on all of God's servants."

The Old Testament prophets longed to understand what God would do in the last days, but they were denied that privilege (1 Peter 1:10). Now, however, in this new dispensation, the apostle Paul tells us that the mystery has been fully revealed by the Spirit to God's holy apostles and prophets in a way that it had not been in previous generations (Ephesians 3:5). The prophetic ministry therefore continues in the church (Ephesians 4:11).

The Bible tells us that we are built on the foundation of the apostles and prophets (Ephesians 2:20). There are two ways in which we can understand this. First, the apostles and prophets laid the foundation at the beginning of the church age and the church is universally and historically built on it. Second, every local church needs to make sure that it is also built on the same apostolic and prophetic foundation. A foundation is a crucial part of a building, though it is later hidden from sight when the structure is completed. What is laid foundationally determines the future shape, size and potential of the building.

Paul wanted to preach where Christ was not known so that he

would not be building on someone else's foundation (Romans 15:20). In addition, in 1 Corinthians 3:10, Paul pointed out that as a wise master builder he "laid a foundation" in the Corinthian church. Laying a foundation in a local church was a dynamic concept which Paul regarded as part of his ministry.

Some time ago I asked a surveyor if I could build a room above my garage. To my surprise, instead of focusing on the appropriate space above the garage, his eyes were fixed on the slab of concrete on which the garage stood. When I told him that I did not want a basement, he laughed and told me that the foundation would determine whether or not I could extend above the existing building. I could not. The foundation was inadequate.

Modern churches are built on all sorts of foundations. Some are built on tradition, some on institution, and some on democracy or sentimentality. In many local churches biblical practices like speaking in tongues are forbidden, because they are foreign to the particular tradition. "You cannot build that here. The foundations will not take it." Radical plans to change the programme can meet with hostility, because people are sentimentally attached to "the way we've always done it here". The unwieldy "majority church vote" can successfully keep such a church rooted in a bygone century. Send a prophet to speak to it and he will be "stoned".

Churches are sometimes built on a predominantly pastoral gift. When this is the case, they run the risk of concentrating on the needs of the flock rather than on the purpose of God. The flock can come to see pastoral care as the key factor of church life. The church can be constantly evaluated on the basis of whether their personal needs are being met rather than whether God's purpose is being fulfilled. For instance, pragmatic changes that should be made in the church programme can be withstood because of undue consideration being given to any discomfort the congregation might face. Thus necessary small-group subdivisions or multiple services might be resisted by a church simply because people express their personal preferences instead of embracing God's guidance for incorporating growth.

If a church is built essentially and exclusively on a teaching gift, it will tend to produce a preaching centre that gathers a crowd but does not build a body. If the major leadership role is in the hands of an evangelist, the local church will reflect the immediacy of his burden for the lost, but again it will not build all that God wants for the local church.

The New Testament teaches that a church will succeed when the vital ministries of pastor, teacher and evangelist are built on an apostolic/prophetic foundation. Without exposure to a prophet, a whole congregation may be Spirit-filled and speaking in tongues, but not know why. Even good churches, if they are not caught up with God's ultimate intention, will find themselves becoming parochial and stagnating instead of reaching the world. The prophet insists on reminding us of our true identity and our calling to make disciples of all the nations. He will not allow us to settle as an inward-looking group.

Churches must be shaped by God's prophetic purpose and remember that we are called to what Christopher Wright calls "The Mission of God", not simply to a local domestic programme. Individual churches will be strengthened in faith for success in their neighbourhood through the encouragement and inspiration of prophetic ministry.

In our early days as a church in Brighton, prophetic foundations were laid, helping us to understand something of our future calling and significance. God promised us, through prophecy, that he had set before us an open door. He also promised us a certain level of visibility that would make us a blessing to the whole town. Years later, when we tried to buy an industrial building and transform it into a worship centre, we were opposed unanimously by the local council. We were also told that perhaps a council decision reached by a small majority of, say, 60 per cent against and 40 per cent for the project might be overturned by an appeal. The reversal of an 80 per cent/20 per cent decision was extremely rare. A 100 per cent refusal was regarded as virtually impossible to change by appeal. We prayed, we appealed, we believed the prophetic promise and we enjoyed the victory which the Lord Jesus gave us as the door swung open and we bought and transformed the building in which we now worship.

God also told us that we would see young people come up through our ranks who would be trained and sent to the nations. Having grown up like shoots among us, he would cut them and fire them out like arrows.

These prophetic utterances have shaped our expectations and church life. We know who we are and what we are called to do. When in Africa recently I spent time with a former university student in Brighton, now leading a church in Ghana and overseeing other churches planted in seven nations in West Africa. He works using insights he gained while with us, and continues enjoying our involvement with him as the churches there grow and develop. Others have been sent to Japan, South Africa, Australia, Canada, the USA and several British towns where churches have been planted.

PROPHETIC ROOTS

When Jeremiah and Ezekiel tried to bring the nation of Israel back to their prophetic roots, they were regarded as enemies of the people. They could not bless what God was not blessing. God is prepared to shake and tear down everything which dishonours Him. He is prepared for the Temple to be destroyed, for the Ark to be stolen, for a television evangelist to be exposed, for His holy name to be dragged through the mud. But He is committed to raising a pure prophetic people who will follow Him wholeheartedly.

Jeremiah prophesied that after seventy years the Israelites would return to the Promised Land. The story of Ezra begins, "… in order to fulfill the word of the Lord by the mouth of Jeremiah…" The nation's recovery programme was rooted in the prophetic word. A new day had dawned! When Haggai later rebuked the people for concentrating more on building their own homes than building the Lord's house, he was speaking relevantly into their situation. They had responded to Jeremiah's prophecy and, since Haggai was building on that foundation, they immediately responded to his reproof.

Churches whose existence and identity have been affected by prophetic foundations can appreciate the ongoing relevance of true prophetic ministry. Local churches are the most natural context for the prophetic ministry, but when churches make no room for this ministry, those with prophetic stirrings will often be tempted to function outside their true sphere. Some gifted prophets who find that they are not received in local churches, have begun to direct their prophetic words to the secular nation, searching, for instance, for "God's prophetic word for the UK". Some will even hope for a latter-day John the Baptist to arise and address No. 10 Downing Street. My conviction is that the prophetic word to pagan Britain today is, "Repent and believe the gospel!" This message is best proclaimed not by an individual prophet, but by a prophetic church living in obedience to God's word.

When Moses told downtrodden, captive Israel that God would soon release them, they were encouraged. Similarly, when today's prophet tells the church, "You are not slaves but sons, not a laughing-stock but a mighty army," Christians rally to the battle cry. The vision lifts their sights. They see afresh the call to go into all the nations.

PROPHETIC GIFTING

The prophet brings direction and exhortation. Haggai told the people to go and get timber for God's house. His message was specific and thoroughly practical. A prophet proves that he is committed to the vision by being the first to respond to it. He leads the march and provides a foundation on which others build.

A prophet brings comfort, consolation and inner fortification. When Israel was overrun by the Babylonians, Habakkuk knew that God was executing His judgment against His people. Yet the prophet also knew that the invaders would be brought to justice at God's appointed time. When Christians are going through pressure, they are comforted by prophecies which explain God's intentions.

A prophet brings solutions. The waters of Marah were bitter until Moses told the people to throw a tree into them (Exodus 15:25). The church must expect God to reveal answers to many of its problems through prophetic gifts.

A prophet motivates action. When the prophets and teachers met to worship and fast at Antioch (Acts 13:1–3), they were not just having a good time of praise. They were concerned with God's prophetic purpose – how to reach the world with the gospel. We should be an active community that is encouraged and strengthened by the prophets (Acts 15:32).

God wants us to weigh prophecy. True prophecy never condemns or crushes us. It is instead something which edifies, exhorts or comforts us. It is always biblical, glorifies Jesus and has an "upward" theme. It builds us up, stirs us up or cheers us up!

If we want to be a prophetic people we must respond to the prophetic word. Once the prophetic stream is moving, God will keep speaking into it. We must take care that we do not throw in defensiveness, hostility or cynicism and thus break the flow. When we hear from God, we need to act and not be taken up with the difficulties that may result. God told the Israelites to go into the Promised Land, but they were more concerned about the giants. Many churches are wandering in the wilderness today because they resisted the prophetic and focused on the problems.

There may be difficulties, but we must respond to the word. God wants to speak to His people and then through them to the world. We need to be captivated by what He says and swift at putting it into practice. Our church should be throbbing with prophetic life and motivated by prophetic vision.

PROPHETIC VISION

"Without vision the people perish." They also get side-tracked into preoccupation with present worries and relative trivialities. Many a congregation contains excellent people, but they are not sufficiently exposed to the prophetic ministry and so fail to be excited by God's ultimate purpose. Short-term problems dominate their thinking and prevent radical change. Even in the midst of spiritual renewal, such congregations fail to grasp what the renewing is for and where God is taking them. The prophet's voice needs to come like an axe to the root of our problems. The prophet has the incisive clarity of vision to cut through rubbish and search out motives and intentions. He forces us to ask uncomfortable questions that lead to uncomfortable answers. He causes the leaders of churches to re-examine their activities in the light of the principles that God has shown them. Often the diagnosis demands drastic surgery that elders would have shrunk from on their own.

The prophet is not simply a preacher, though he will preach. He is not simply an expositor of the Bible, though his great burden is to bring us back to the Bible and its authority.

Prophets bring people revelation and clarity concerning God's purpose for their time. Jeremiah, for instance, had to burst the balloon of false trust in outward religion, calling Judah to true dependence on God, not just on his Temple (Jeremiah 7:4). While they continued depending on their traditions as if they had all the time in the world, Jeremiah had to warn them that their time was rapidly running out.

The prophet must have room not only to speak at large conferences, but also to come into our churches. We must be prepared for him to expose our weaknesses so that we might change.

Clarity of vision keeps us from activity that is not centred on the ultimate goal. When the vision of the kingdom of God fills our horizon it will affect our whole lifestyle, our values and our decisions. As a young Christian I was taught no true vision for the church. Raised on dispensationalism, I was told that we were living in the Laodicean age and the Lord's return was our only hope. The whole emphasis of my evangelical life was "personal". I had a "personal" Saviour, practised "personal" evangelism and pursued "personal" devotions. No one told me that God had promised His Son the nations as His inheritance and the ends of the earth as His possession (Psalm 2:8), or that the increase of His government would know no end (Isaiah 9:7), or that the saints of the Most High would receive the kingdom and possess it for ever (Daniel 7:18), or that these glorious promises somehow included me!

Though our church was keen on missionary work, it was never taught that "He will bring forth justice to the nations… He will not be disheartened or crushed until He has established justice in the earth; and the coastlands will wait expectantly for His law" (Isaiah 42:1, 4). By contrast, missionary work consisted of isolated stabs at Satan's strongholds.

Now, however, we are beginning to understand the great implications of God's magnificent prophetic statements for the church and for the nations of the world. People's lives have been changed by encountering and embracing prophetic vision. Within our ranks there are those who have turned down promotion for the sake of the kingdom and have been willing to jeopardize their career if to advance it meant being transferred to a place where there was no kingdom activity.

Some have tried to dismiss the prophetic gift by arguing that a prophet is simply a preacher or teacher, but the lists of gifts in Ephesians 4:11, 1 Corinthians 12:28 and Romans 12:6–7 are consistent in differentiating between them. Why does the Holy Spirit record them as different if they are simply the same gift, and what are we missing in the church without their ministry?

Listening to a prophet is not like listening to a teacher. The prophet will sometimes sound unbalanced. For a while he will sound as though he has only one message. His burden will not be to make sure that the balance is correct, but that the present issue is being resolved. It will be the local elders' responsibility to work out the detailed implications of the grand sweep of the prophetic vision. Often his insights will need the wisdom of apostolic ministry to bring the balance necessary to build safely for the future. Prophetic vision in tandem with apostolic wisdom is a powerful combination from the living God to build living churches.

CHAPTER 13

THE CRUCIAL ROLE OF LEADERSHIP

If the church is perceived as simply a gathering of people who attend religious services, little leadership is required. Leading the meetings and preaching sermons are all that must be mastered. If, however, the church is seen in a different light, namely as the focal point of God's purposes for world evangelization and the key centre for discipleship, training, envisioning and releasing ministry, then leadership takes on a totally new meaning.

Leaders are needed who will genuinely inspire a following by their godly character and charismatic gifting. Good leaders are worth their weight in gold. Christians count it a privilege to follow them. The ascended Christ is determined to have a mature and well-functioning church and to accomplish this He has made anointed leadership a top priority. He has ascended on high and has given some to be apostles, some prophets, some evangelists, and some pastors and teachers.

God-given leadership provides security, motivation and direction. A leader who knows he is genuinely called and loved by God brings peace and security to a local church. He gives identity and a sense of destiny to the congregation. He also stirs motivation. God's people are often conscious of their need of motivation. They greatly value a leader who can fan into a flame the fire that can sometimes become dull in their souls. Left to themselves they often feel casual and indifferent, but they can be stirred to enthusiastic action by a charismatic leader.

The vision given to a leader when he is called by God should shape his ministry. Those who follow him will be gripped by his dream and expectation. Such developments are often shown in Scripture. Paul testified that he was not disobedient to the vision impressed on him when God apprehended him. It shaped his life and subsequently the lives of others like Timothy, who got caught up in his magnificent obsession. God calls and anoints leaders and then gathers others to their anointing. Perhaps David's example can serve to illustrate:

> *Then all the tribes of Israel came to David at Hebron and said, "Behold, we are your bone and your flesh. Previously, when Saul was king over us, you were the one who led Israel out and in and the Lord said to you, 'You will shepherd My people Israel, and you will be a ruler over Israel.'" So all the elders of Israel came to the king at Hebron, and King David made a covenant with them before the Lord at Hebron; then they anointed David king over Israel.*
> (2 **Samuel** 5:1–3)

ONE OF US

In David's anointing for leadership several principles can be observed. First, the people said to him, "We are your bone and your flesh." It is vital that a true leader is a man of the people, known and loved by them. He is not a stranger or professional outsider.

The kind of mystique associated with some people's concepts of priesthood keeps the "man of God" away from the people. David was their "flesh and blood". Biblical elders were chosen from among the people, not from the distant theological college. Theological study is not to be despised, but wrong concepts of church leadership must be challenged. Too often men have been encouraged to take theological training before they have shown any proof of gifting and calling, and certainly college provides neither.

Charles Simpson tells the following story. He was working at a part-time job when a large, happy, gregarious black lady stopped him as he swept the floor and asked:

> *"You're new around here, ain't you?"*
> *"Yes I am."*
> *"You go to college?"* she pressed.
> *"Yes I do."*
> *"What are you studying?"* she asked.
> *"Well…"* I was not prepared for examination and my answer must have sounded tentative. *"Well I am studying to be a preacher."*
> She laughed loudly. *"Boy, you don't study to be no preacher. Either you is or you ain't!"*

(Charles Simpson, *The Challenge to Care*, Vine Books, 1986)

If a man has been called and gifted, however, some training can be of great value. My problem is more with the system that produces an annual crop of ministers from its colleges who are then ordained into their denominations' ministry and thereby regarded as "ministers". As such they then "find a church", arriving as trained professionals. Such ministers initially have no relationship with the churches they are sent to, but are regarded as their leaders.

Leadership doesn't work like this. David's people knew him. He was bone of their bone. In Paul's day elders were appointed from within the flock. Timothy and Titus were not sent from outside by Paul to become church elders, but were to appoint elders from within local churches. The Holy Spirit made overseers from among the flock and they were the church's shepherds (Acts 20).

Those appointing David could say to him, "Previously, when Saul was king over us, you were the one who led Israel out and in" (2 Samuel 5:2). David had shown clear gifting. Even when in a junior position his God-given ability was known by the people who were now about to make him their leader. He was no stranger to them; he did not come with mere paper qualifications. When Paul laid hands on elders in the New Testament churches, or when he sent Titus or Timothy to take their responsibility on his behalf, he would appoint known and gifted men.

Some modern denominations have a policy of moving their

ministers from place to place with great speed so that they never form relationships with their people. I was once addressing a large ministers' conference in South Africa and the leader of the denomination told me he moved ministers from church to church every two or three years. When asked why, he explained that they would have given all they had to give after two or three years. No time was given to forming relationships, so the pastors became the loneliest people in the church (except for their wives, who were often lonelier...).

How can we build loving communities of deeply integrated people if the leader himself is a stranger in our midst? His appeal to people on the edges of the church to become more involved can sound rather hollow when everybody knows that he, the pastor, is the biggest "outsider" in the place. He knows nobody and nobody knows him beyond the extent of his professional pastoral relationships with them.

HIS CALLING

Next, those appointing David made reference to his own personal calling. They knew that God had said to him, "You will shepherd My people Israel." They had confidence he was God's man living under the influence of God's personal call. He would not be simply a man-made appointment with a man-pleasing agenda. He had promises from God burning in his heart; he had a secret experience with God; he had the powerful anointing by Samuel in his history. Now he was coming to true spiritual government with a deep sense of commissioning in his soul.

No man can take spiritual leadership to himself. If he is not called and commissioned by God, why should anybody follow him? But if he is, he needs freedom to lead from the front. Democratic structures, committees and boards represent a totally different form of church leadership – one which is unknown in the Bible. Anointing and calling are God's way of maintaining His government in His church. Christ ascended on high. He gave gifts of leadership.

Israel succeeded as a nation when it was led by called and

anointed leaders. Charismatic leadership is God's gift to the church. He chooses whom He anoints with gifts of leadership so He retains His rule. When God anoints someone, His anointing becomes apparent to all. The spiritual gifting that is demonstrated as a result of the anointing gives public profile to the individual concerned. Often gifting in preaching or communicating the word begins to demonstrate God's hand upon a man. This gives him a sphere of influence, and people begin to realize that they hear God through this man – he seems to bring God nearer to them. If his character and leadership skills match this public skill in the word of God, people begin to gather to him for spiritual leadership. This is a spiritual development, not an institutional one. As his vision, leadership skills and ability to communicate bear fruit in lives, people become joined to him like people did to David. They begin to speak as those who said to David: "We are yours, O David."

Some Christians become nervous at this point, uneasy about the personal nature of this commitment, but God builds churches by joining people together in love and trust and personal loyalty, as well as individual devotion to Jesus. Paul testified, "they gave themselves first to the Lord and then to us" (2 Corinthians 8:5 NIV). When men gave themselves to David, the Bible does not see this as a mistake or a fleshly rush of enthusiasm. In fact it records that the statement was made by men upon whom the Holy Spirit had come, and it was He who inspired their spoken commitment (1 Chronicles 12:18). David in turn received them and appointed them to positions of authority according to their gifting. Thus God's anointing on David was the prevailing factor in the forming of the people. David was anointed to lead; others responded to that gifting and yielded themselves to its influence. The men who did this were not weaklings or "yes men"; the Bible makes it plain that they were powerful in their own right. Their exploits were legendary, their courage was clear for all to see. These tough, fearless individuals found great joy in submitting their lives to David's God-given leadership skill, so that they too could enjoy the benefits of the prophetic promises that shaped David's life.

A GOD-GIVEN SPHERE

Next, notice that David ruled in a God-given sphere – God had called him to rule over Israel. His sphere was the whole nation. That was God's calling upon him; he did not snatch it. Indeed, he had waited patiently throughout Saul's rule, but now he entered into what God had planned for him. Now, by God's will, he was to lead Israel.

The New Testament church was told, "Obey your leaders" (Hebrews 13:17); "respect those who... are over you in the Lord" (1 Thessalonians 5:12 NIV). These spiritual principles of leadership must be in place. It is difficult to apply these principles in an institutional situation. If a leader is simply a denominational appointment and shows none of the leadership characteristics described in the Bible, it is very difficult to say, "We are yours." If the man lacks calling, anointing, vision and motivation, nothing stirs you inwardly to express your commitment. Loyalty has to be inspired and earned.

Institutional Christianity does not produce this kind of chemistry. One British national newspaper described a minister as "a general dogsbody looking after a group of well-meaning but harmless people". Obviously this is not always the case, but it is often the way our media portray things and it sometimes feels like the truth.

LAYING ON OF HANDS

Finally, in the account of David's appointment comes the actual covenant between ruler and people and the further anointing to fulfil the ministry. Thus in the New Testament all preparation leads up to actual laying on of hands for recognized responsibility. Surely at this point further anointing is given to the publicly recognized shepherd of the flock and the people are publicly acknowledging their willing desire for him to lead them.

New Testament elders are always referred to in the plural. The anointed leader of a work does not stand alone but as an elder among elders. In a small work plurality might prove impossible.

It may be that only one so far shows evidence of God's anointing on him. We should not rush into laying hands on anyone suddenly (1 Timothy 5:22) simply to make up numbers and prove we are biblical, but we must expect the biblical norm of plurality to emerge. No one should be co-opted when there is no proof of gifting or calling. Appointments without gifting will soon turn the church into a cold institution. If a man is not called or gifted but holds office, he is simply an appointment, and we begin to drift away from biblical norms into religious externality.

Those appointed by God into positions of leadership in the church have a high calling. They not only teach the word and lead the people, they also set the tone of the church. They create its atmosphere and style and establish its philosophy of ministry. Their own sense of calling and destiny provides security, motivation and direction to the church. It is, therefore, difficult to overstate the key role of leadership and its charismatic nature.

We should not be surprised to note a great contrast between churches led by genuine, anointed leaders who are loved, valued, respected and given freedom to lead, and churches where democracy rules. Boards and committees, elections and voting are unknown in Scripture. There must come a rediscovery of biblical norms where the Holy Spirit calls and equips leadership and where that leadership is given room to operate.

PRAYERFUL BRAINSTORMING

This does not mean that times of prayerful brainstorming and discussion are inappropriate. In Acts 15 we see a time of tension in the early church over the matter of circumcision. It was resolved through discussion and godly interaction. In conclusion the elders and apostles present were able to send a message to all the churches which represented their united decision. They said, "It seemed good to the Holy Spirit and to us" (Acts 15:28).

Several men shared their perspectives. Scriptures were quoted, examples from their previous experience were noted. Finally James spoke with an authority which satisfied all who were present and his perspective was happily owned by everybody. In all of this their preoccupation was to ensure that they were genuinely obeying the Holy Spirit and not simply seeing what the majority felt. They were deeply conscious that they were serving God in His church and that the Holy Spirit was among them to lead.

As a young Christian I was invited to become a member of my local Baptist church. I had been blessed and built up there through the faithful teaching of the godly pastor. Having attended for a few years and been baptized, I was told that if I became a member, I could attend the church business meetings and even vote on issues and decisions facing the church.

As a comparatively inexperienced believer I followed the advice given, but I can only say that when I actually attended the "business meeting" I was profoundly shocked by its atmosphere. It was vastly different from the Sunday services where the pastor's God-given skills and obvious spiritual authority enriched all who were present. Here, he was addressed as an employee with no more authority than anyone else. Angry people "proposed", others "seconded". Hands and voices were raised, not in worship and acknowledgment of the Holy Spirit's presence, but in an endeavour to make sure that personal preferences were heard. Prayer had been a formal preliminary. This, it seems, was democracy at work. As a spiritually unqualified young believer, I could have my vote and it had as much authority as that of the pastor who had served the church for years. I was dismayed!

Where tradition is the entrenched norm, and democratic power is held by a majority who treasure the past, we should not be surprised to note little freedom of movement or spiritual progress. When the Holy Spirit says, "Behold, I do a new thing," sadly the democratic vote will often reply, "Not here, you won't."

SPIRITUAL AUTHORITY

Spiritual authority. The words send a shiver down many a Christian spine! Yet when correctly handled, true spiritual authority creates security, peace and real joy in the Holy Spirit. Everything depends upon how it is handled.

The only time that Jesus particularly pointed out to His disciples that He was their Master and Lord was as He disrobed, took a towel and, as a servant, washed their feet. He did it as an example, a visual aid. It would be for ever inscribed upon their memories. Many years later, Peter was writing to elders and reminding them to be examples and not to lord it over the flock. "Clothe yourselves with humility," he continued, doubtless reflecting on that unforgettable night.

Jesus contrasted His kingdom with the world when He said, "You know that the rulers of the Gentiles lord it over them, and their high officials exercise authority over them. Not so with you. Instead, whoever wants to become great among you must be your servant" (Matthew 20:25–26 NIV).

The restoration of spiritual authority opens a way fraught with dangers. How easy to take hold of verses and drive them to false conclusions! How easy to lust for positions of prestige and power where authority can be exercised! How easy to miss totally the Spirit of Christ! There are real dangers and there have undoubtedly been abuses, but this must not drive us away from God-given principles. Leaders must have freedom to lead the church, or we shall never advance.

Close inspection reveals what style that leadership should adopt. Writing to the Thessalonians, Paul said, "we were gentle among you, like a mother caring for her little children… as a father deals with his own children" (1 Thessalonians 2:7, 11 NIV). He addressed the Philippians as "my brothers, you whom I love and long for" (Philippians 4:1 NIV). And to the Corinthians he said, "I am not writing this to shame you, but to warn you, as my dear children" (1 Corinthians 4:14 NIV). Nursing mother, father, brothers, children – they are all intimate family terms.

MEEKNESS AND GENTLENESS

When the apostle spoke to the churches, he was led by "the meekness and gentleness of Christ" (2 Corinthians 10:1). Although he used strong language in very serious situations, he more often implored the believers to hear him and encouraged others to adopt this same loving attitude. "If someone is caught in a sin, you who are spiritual should restore him gently" (Galatians 6:1 NIV), he said, and advocated the same spirit of gentleness towards those who opposed "sound teaching" (2 Timothy 2:24–25).

Paul did not order the Corinthians, "Do this!" Rather, he appealed to their wisdom: "I speak to sensible people; judge for yourselves what I say" (1 Corinthians 10:15 NIV). He did not bully the weak, but became weak in order to win them (1 Corinthians 9:22). This is the Spirit of Christ in operation and God longs to see it motivating His church.

The fact is that spiritual authority only operates properly where people have happily yielded themselves to it. It cannot be forced upon the unwilling. Hearts must first be won and trust be gained. We have seen that the men who joined David's growing army said, "We are yours." These new recruits had come to love and respect David. They wholeheartedly gave him their allegiance. David did not have to argue for his authority but could rest in the fact that, not unlike Jesus, all that the Father had given him would come to him.

A man who often contends for his own authority is actually betraying the fact that he is insecure in that role.

A TIME TO CORRECT

Confrontation is an important responsibility for all church leaders, since it guards the flock of God against error. If, however, correction is more frequent than encouragement, people have great difficulty receiving it. God wants His shepherds to relate to the flock as friends. When people know they are loved, they will often receive words that will hurt, because they believe that "faithful are the wounds of a friend" (Proverbs 27:6).

Correction must be done with love. A surgeon has one goal: to make his patient well again. However, he knows that there is a right time and place for the operation – he doesn't lop something off as he passes his patient in the corridor. And he knows that he must prepare himself – he doesn't turn up drunk and disorderly at the operating theatre!

If there is a problem with someone in the church, we do not put the matter off for two years, but neither do we say, "It's about time I spoke to him," and plunge in the knife! We react in a spirit of gentleness: "This is a delicate operation. I've got to prepare myself and pray for the right moment and setting. God, help me to express love."

BUILDING UP

The purpose of all spiritual authority is to bless and build up the flock of God. It should be the outworking of the love and devotion of the leadership to the people. There should grow a developing expression of love. Paul said to the Corinthians that they did not have many fathers. God is looking for fatherly love from leadership towards the flock.

One of the goals of parents is to create within their children the ability to make wise decisions. Sadly, some parents fail at this because they dominate their children. They give commands instead of counsel, orders instead of training and scolding instead of correction, thereby producing insecurity and low self-worth in their offspring. Church leaders must avoid the same dangers.

Jesus said, "The kings of the Gentiles lord it over them… But you are not to be like that" (Luke 22:25–26 NIV). The leader who dominates will become suspicious of the people, particularly when they come up with new ideas. "Jim's got another wonderful plan for the worship meeting!" the leader will grumble, and feel threatened. Creative thinkers can be regarded as enemies. In time, the leader will communicate to the people, "We don't want anyone here to think, thank you," frustrating those who have a valuable contribution to make. A possessive attitude in a leader will stifle people's genuine expression of loyalty and make them suspicious. Leaders must not fear the people and prevent them from offering their contributions. I am only too ready to admit that some of the best things we have developed in *Newfrontiers* have not come from my personal initiatives. And some of the major changes at Church of Christ the King in

Brighton have come about in response to prophecies that other people have given. We can all hear and contribute.

Spiritual authority does not eradicate the wisdom of the body but draws on it. Paul says, "Not that we lord it over your faith, but we work with you for your joy" (2 Corinthians 1:24 NIV). Leaders are there not to dominate others' faith, but to help them to be joyful and fulfilled. Leaders do not force people to recognize their spiritual authority. They lead by example. Paul did not say to Timothy, "Let no man despise your youth – show them who's boss!" Instead, he exhorted him to set an example to the believers "in life, in love, in faith and in purity" (1 Timothy 4:12 NIV).

A PEACEFUL CONSCIENCE

Paul said, "we commend ourselves to every man's conscience in the sight of God" (2 Corinthians 4:2 NIV). Leaders can be knowledgeable and eloquent, but if they cannot commend themselves to people's consciences they will not be followed. People want leaders whom they know to be godly, trustworthy and transparent. If leaders do commend themselves to their people's conscience, then, in spite of their weakness and vulnerability, they will find their people following happily.

If a leader's character must appeal to people's conscience, so must his words. A young man told me that his pastor had said to him, "I believe that you should move closer to the church and that your wife should give up her job to look after the children." The young man asked me, "If we don't do these things, are we disobeying God?"

"No," I replied. "If you do something just because you are told to, you are not combining your action with faith. If, in a few weeks' time, you find yourself in debt, you will blame your pastor. Leadership cannot force its will. This man has brought you his counsel and now he wants you to pray about it. If his advice witnesses with your conscience, God will give you faith for it. Only when you are convinced that God has told you to do something can you commit yourself to it with faith. You must give full weight to your pastor's counsel, but you must also arrive at your own faith."

This same principle can work in another way. A church member may come to the leadership and say, "God is calling me to the mission field and I want to join 'X' missionary society." But the group of leaders may feel uneasy and advise him not to proceed. So now what happens? Does this mean he is forbidden to advance? Is he a rebel if he ignores counsel?

No. Leaders must appeal to the individual's conscience, to his walk with God. They must say, "We do not have faith for this. We cannot go beyond our conscience, but neither can we force our will on you."

If he is then accepted by the missionary society, he must be free to proceed, but he in turn must not expect the leaders of the church publicly to lay hands upon him and send him, for he has proceeded on his own initiative. Leaders must not feel obliged to lay hands on all who feel that they are called to the mission field. Leaders can still express their love and care to the intended missionary, but they must not go beyond their own faith by laying hands upon him if they doubt his call. In the end, time will prove who was right. This procedure can be followed with genuine openness of heart and love.

ROOM TO BREATHE

Spiritual authority must leave room to breathe and must never dominate people's lives. Once leaders have offered their counsel, they must give people space – the chance to find out for themselves what God is saying.

God may do the most extraordinary things through certain individuals, even when they seem to break every rule in the book! But there will still be those who return in six months and say, "I'm sorry. I got it wrong. I didn't listen." If this happens they don't need to be treated like rebels. Rather, the church should reaffirm their love for them and joyfully welcome them back.

If the leadership holds things too tightly, the church will never make the extraordinary and spontaneous breakthroughs that seem to characterize the book of Acts. There we see Philip suddenly going to the Samaritans, Peter amazingly going to Cornelius' home without first checking with the other apostles, and Ananias going to see the hated and feared Saul just because the Spirit told him to go. Some of the most amazing advances in the book of Acts come when individuals respond to the personal promptings of the Holy Spirit. They are not the result of cleverly strategized movements coming from recognised and appointed leadership.

In reality, any sensitive member of the body of Christ can hear the Holy Spirit and respond to His promptings.

WILLING TO BE ACCOUNTABLE

It is important to note, however, that Philip was more than willing to give an account of his work in Samaria to Peter and John when they came from Jerusalem to see what God was doing through his ministry there. Philip did not withstand their enquiries, insisting that this was *his* sphere of service. Rather, he allowed Peter and John to bring their apostolic wisdom to his evangelistic initiative.

Also, Peter was willing to answer the enquiries of the other apostles when they asked questions about his going to the Gentile Cornelius. He did not simply argue that he as an individual had full freedom to do whatever he liked. He was more than willing, having obeyed the Holy Spirit, to then work out his accountability to the other apostles by making full explanation of why he had gone to a Gentile home and baptized Gentiles.

In the early church there was freedom to respond to individual promptings of the Holy Spirit, but also a genuine sense of accountability and spiritual authority, so the mighty New Testament church moved on in power and security.

God has given spiritual authority for our safety and protection. There is plenty of room for diversity of gift, but God wants us to be united in spirit and to know those who are over us in the Lord. The goal of every church leader is to produce mature, outgoing, well-relating people who can cope with pressure and build secure relationships. The leader's goal is like Paul's, namely to present everyone mature, not everyone dependent.

In reality, a truly mature person does not withstand the counsel of others. Aware of his own limitations and blind spots, he is grateful to God for those who love him sufficiently to bring him counsel and admonition. He will be aware that he can be misled and ensnared by the devil and so will be grateful for the checks and balances which spiritual authority provides.

Do you enjoy the benefits of accountability to someone in the body of Christ? Do you know and appreciate those who are over you in the Lord (1 Thessalonians 5:12)?

Beware the dangers of the "lone ranger" mentality – well-intentioned, perhaps, but answerable to no one. Find your place in a local church and develop relationships with responsible leadership so that you can grow and be helped towards Christian maturity.

You will learn to give thanks for God's gift of spiritual authority.

CHAPTER 14

THE CHURCH THROUGH AN APOSTLE'S EYES

Jesus revolutionized the thinking of His contemporaries when He taught them to call God "Father". To them, God had been distant and fearful, not intimate and knowable. Jesus assured His followers that their heavenly Father knew their needs and delighted in meeting them. He introduced a "family atmosphere" to prayer. The new community He formed enjoyed intimacy with God and with one another.

Following Jesus' example, Paul and the other early apostles laid a foundation of love and friendship in the churches by their style. They were not remote rabbis or distant church growth experts. Paul came among the churches as a father, and when he left them they wept. When he wrote to them he addressed them in the tenderest terms.

The world around us longs for intimacy. People look for love and are bewildered by their experiences. They feel let down, used, robbed and spoiled. In this computer age they lack personal significance and value. Is there no one at home in the universe? The gospel not only tells us that there is a God in heaven, but also that there is a family on earth to which we can belong, and that there are leaders who know how to build not remote, faceless congregations but loving, caring communities.

When I was first converted I found it extremely difficult to penetrate church life as it was then expressed. It seemed so formal and distant. Obviously comparative strangers, people greeted one another at the door with correct handshakes. Actually they only seemed to shake one person's hand, and that was the pastor's as they left the building. Formal clothing, solid pews, old-fashioned music, hushed atmosphere, unreal antiquated language – all conspired to alienate me rather than welcome me to this new and frightening territory. Gradually I learned how to conduct myself and was taught the "language of Zion". Little by little the metamorphosis was taking place. I guessed that this was what it meant to be a Christian. It was all new to me, so I had to knuckle down and learn.

At the same time other longings were striving in my heart. Surely the good friendships I had enjoyed with my ungodly friends in the world should be surpassed in the church. If this is God's family, shouldn't it be better, richer and more meaningful, instead of unreal, religious and distant? It was so different in the Bible.

If we are going to reach our generation with the gospel and build churches that are relevant to our contemporaries and true to Scripture, we must rediscover the style of New Testament Christianity. The tone adopted by each of the apostles when writing their letters to the churches they served sets a great standard. Tenderness and affection are mixed with undoubted spiritual authority.

GENUINE BROTHERS

When Paul wrote to his friends at Philippi, he communicated so much of God's attitude and was transparent about his own feelings for them. He wrote to them as his brothers, his beloved, his longed for, his joy and his crown (Philippians 4:1). Though Paul was a mighty apostle and arguably the greatest Christian leader of all time, he addressed the Christians at Philippi first as his "brothers". No clergy/laity divide in Paul's mind. Although he argued in 1 Corinthians 12 that "God has set in the church first apostles", he did not stand aloof. In the church of Jesus Christ all are brothers! Jesus Himself introduced the wonder of this new relationship when

He said, "Go instead to my brothers and tell them, 'I am returning to my Father and your Father, to my God and your God'" (John 20:17 NIV). He isn't ashamed to call us brothers (Hebrews 2:11); he is the firstborn among many brothers (Romans 8:29). Brothers can relax together and joke together, and they do not even have to call one another "brother Terry" or "brother John". I have four sons and I have never heard one of them call another "brother Tim" or "brother Simon".

As Rob Warner has said, "There are still churches where first names are never mentioned in the notices. Collecting the offering has the formal precision of a military exercise, and communion is distributed with the co-ordinated stiffness and unreality of a synchronised swimming team" (Rob Warner, *21st Century Church*, Hodder & Stoughton, 1993).

My former pastor was shocked that I refused to wear a clerical collar and amazed that I invited the church members to call me by my Christian name. He feared I would earn no respect from my congregation if I did not retain the normal trappings of the ministry. At Bible college I was told I should not form friendships with anyone in the congregation. If I wanted a friend I should seek out a pastor in a neighbouring town! "Distance yourself!" But God wants a family that is built on loving relationships.

More recently pastors have been increasingly impressed by the successful growth of businesses and the methods used by business leaders to promote growth. This has often led to a pragmatism foreign to the atmosphere of the Bible. Professionals are hired as so-called "staff members" and assessed on their accomplishments, and if necessary are fired, as in a business, if their work rate or stats don't impress, rather than being recognized as elders emerging among the flock.

Churches can sometimes become obsessed with numbers, so that members feel that they are merely a means to an end and not particularly valued for themselves. Growth can be measured purely in terms of the body count on Sundays while spiritual growth and developing maturity can be marginalized or go unnoticed.

Of course, numerical growth is not something to be ignored or treated with indifference. Paul celebrated growth and Jesus has ambition to win the nations for His inheritance. Numbers matter. Healthy bodies should grow in size.

The church should demonstrate wholehearted commitment to reaching the vast crowds of unreached people, and this will require concentrated effort.

HEARTFELT LOVE

Paul called the Philippians "my beloved". No embarrassment clouded the issue. He loved them and wanted them to know it. It is wonderful to be loved and to have the liberty to express love to others. Do you ever tell other believers that you love them? I do not mean in that unreal way in which charismatics are sometimes called upon by the meeting leader to turn to the person sitting next to them and repeat, parrot-like, some terms of endearment. I am told that the sadly missed David Watson was once in a meeting where all present were exhorted to turn to their immediate neighbour with the words, "I can't live without you." He turned and discovered to his dismay that he was standing next to a very beautiful blonde young woman. He could not bring himself to express the required declaration of personal devotion!

There are, nevertheless, many opportunities when believers can plainly tell others of their love. Paul frequently did so and called God to be his witness on one occasion (see 2 Corinthians 11:11). Relationships of love modelled by leaders are of enormous value in setting the style for church life. Many in the modern world feel terribly unloved. It is wonderful when we can honestly express our heartfelt love to one another – not as sentimental, superficial jargon, but out of developing relationships of trust, appreciation, respect and delight.

LONGED FOR

Paul longed for his friends at Philippi. He called them "my longed for". He had zealous ambition for them; he longed to see them, be with them, inspire their progress, help them stand. He longed for them not simply from his own human resources of affection, but with the passion of Christ. In the opening remarks of his letter he spoke of experiencing longings for them with all the inner yearnings of Christ (Philippians 1). Christ's love and zeal for them were burning in Paul's heart.

This kind of language is far removed from much modern church life, where correctness and balance prevail and cordial affection has replaced passion. If we keep opening our hearts to the Holy Spirit, He will pour God's love into them, rekindling the kind of love that He so desires in His church. Wholehearted love is His desired norm. He wants nothing less in our ranks. Lukewarmness is anathema to Him. He is sickened by it.

MY JOY

Next, Paul saw them as his "joy". He delighted in them. He did not constantly complain about the shortcomings of the churches he served. Rather, he commended them and flooded them with affection and grace. We might argue that it was one thing to rejoice over the Philippian church, but what about others, like Corinth? Was he equally affirming about all the churches? To our surprise, we discover that before he corrected the wayward Corinthians he first affirmed them and rejoiced in their lacking no gift. He did not correct them in order to shame them, but rather to exhort them as his dear children. They had many tutors but not many fathers. If to others he was not an apostle, he was to them. He calls them "the proof" of his apostolic ministry.

Imagine citing the Corinthian church as proof of your apostleship! Here was a church involved in incest, drunkenness at the Lord's Table, divisiveness, carnality, wrong handling of charismatic gifts, pride and more, but Paul called them the proof of his apostolic ministry! He owned them and loved them, even though he longed for them to change. He did not disown them; they were his children in the Lord. They also, like Philippi, were his joy.

It is so easy for Christian leaders to create the wrong ethos in the church. Constant exhortations and heavy-handed manipulation become the norm in some congregations. Many languish under a cloud of condemnation intensified by preaching, which only adds burdens. Many a believer is crushed by a vague sense of inadequacy, of not producing enough or not being worthy of God's affirmation. How believers need to hear the kind of unequivocal statements that Paul loved to shout from the house-tops; namely, that nothing can separate us from the love of Christ! If God is for us, who is against us (Romans 8:31)? Many believers desperately need to know for certain what the psalmist knew when he joyfully said, "This I know – God is for me!" (Psalm 56:9).

The church is God's joy. She is the joy of all the earth (Psalm 48:2). First God tells us what we are by His grace – His joy! Then He helps us to live accordingly. Grace lifts us, stirs hope in our hearts and inspires us to rise to our calling.

MY CROWN

Finally Paul described the Philippians as his "crown". Not a royal crown, but a wreath of victory, something gained at the winning post. Paul always saw life in the context of "prize day" before Christ at His coming. He constantly referred to that day when Christ would appear. His desire was to present a pure virgin to Christ; to present every man mature in Him. They were his crown of rejoicing in that day!

With this in mind, Paul urged those in his care to press on with all diligence. He did not see them as his short-term responsibility. He was not coldly professional – he saw himself as joined to people for the whole duration. Even when absent, he held them in his heart. Paul looked forward to the crown. When writing to Timothy he had almost finished his course. He was not overwhelmed with nostalgia for the "good old days"; he was still looking forward. Having said he had finished the course, his next few words were not "in the past", but "in the future"!

When Paul called the church at Philippi his "crown" he was thinking of the future. In Philippians 2:16 he told them to hold fast to the word of life so that in the day of Christ he might have cause to glory because he did not run in vain or toil in vain. To the Thessalonians he said, "For who is our hope or joy or crown of exultation? Is it not even you, in the presence of our Lord Jesus at His coming?" (1 Thessalonians 2:19).

Paul was no time server or hireling. He was profoundly joined to those he cared for. They had lasting significance for him and he could not afford to play at religion. The progress of those in his charge mattered deeply. He was looking for the crown and in a mysterious way his crown was related to their progress and their ultimate success.

Many modern Christians have heard little about rewards, and rarely think of the great day of their presentation before Christ. Not so Paul. He kept that day in constant focus. He believed in rewards. His life service came before Ignatius of Loyola's famous prayer, "Not looking for any reward save that of knowing I do thy will." This may be a fine-sounding sentiment, but it simply isn't a biblical one. Jesus said, "I am coming soon! My reward is with me, and I will give to everyone according to what he has done" (Revelation 22:12 NIV). It is not for you to be slightly embarrassed about the whole concept of rewards. It is hardly your place to correct Jesus and tell Him that rewards are rather a shallow ethic and that you have risen above such things. Jesus wants to share the spoils of His victory and is committed to rewarding your works.

Paul knew that everything in this life was by grace, but God's grace was not in vain in his case, since it motivated him to labour "harder than all of them" (1 Corinthians 15:10 NIV). Paul's own example of passion and zeal helped to set the tone for the churches of his day. As a good leader he was always pressing on, longing to lay hold of that for which God had laid hold of him, not regarding himself as having arrived but pressing forward (Philippians 3).

Leaders should provide an atmosphere of love and security, of affirmation and acceptance, of brotherly love and mutual delight, but they should also bring a sense of passionate commitment to Christ's cause. Christ wants a glorious and magnificent bride. Paul was determined to play his part in preparing one. He wanted the churches he served to be similarly passionate about the coming wedding day.

The presentation day consumed Paul's vision. He communicated that zeal not only in the grand sweep of his massive vision of the universal church, but by helping a group of believers at Philippi to understand that they also were part of it all. They were his brothers, his beloved, his longed for, his joy and crown.

Although Paul was the outstanding apostle of the New Testament, his attitudes are not to be regarded as unique. This former cold-hearted Pharisee had been transformed by an encounter with Christ. Filled with the Holy Spirit, he became a channel of God's love to the churches. You can experience the same transformation. The Holy Spirit can flood your heart with love for other believers. Your church can be a centre of love, joy and delight. Forgiven much, you can learn to give away mercy freely. As the Holy Spirit is poured out in your church, you see how much God loves His people and treasures them in spite of their obvious weaknesses and failures. Become a giver of love in your church. Help it to become a place of love and peace – the loving family that people are longing to find.

CHAPTER 15

THE WORK OF AN APOSTLE

Can we dispense with apostles today? We may arrive at a variety of conclusions if we simply pool our own ideas. If we yield to the Bible, however, we shall find the true answer.

What is an apostle? The Greek word for apostle has its root in the verb "to send", so apostle basically means "a sent one". Jesus repeatedly referred to Himself as one, having been sent from the Father. Bishop Lightfoot tells us in his commentary on Galatians that the apostle is "not only the messenger but the delegate of the person who sends him. He is entrusted with a mission and has powers conferred upon him" (J. B. Lightfoot, *St Paul's Epistle to the Galatians*, Macmillan, 1981, p. 94).

THREE CLASSES

We can distinguish three classes of apostle in the New Testament. First of all there is Jesus, "the Apostle and High Priest of our confession" (Hebrews 3:1). Next there are "the twelve". Some feel that this is the end of the story, and that Paul was raised up by God to replace Judas. It is argued that we never hear of the hastily appointed Matthias again; but actually we never hear of many of the twelve again, and the Bible nowhere states that Paul was one of the twelve. He clearly distinguishes himself from them in 1 Corinthians 15:5–8. The twelve were "apostles of the Lamb" (Revelation 21:14), called by Jesus during His earthly ministry. The replacement for Judas had to be one who had accompanied them from the beginning.

It could almost be argued that Paul is in a category of his own as "one untimely born" (1 Corinthians 15:8). He was certainly given an extraordinary amount of revelation to contribute to the Scriptures. He was, nevertheless, commissioned by the ascended Christ, and must therefore be regarded as generally belonging to the category referred to in Ephesians 4:8–11, where we read that "He ascended on high... and He gave some as apostles".

Special pleading might also be made for James, the brother of Jesus (Galatians 1:19), who emerged as a leading apostle even though he seems to have been an unbeliever during Jesus' earthly ministry. In the council at Jerusalem he seems to have obtained an even more influential place than Paul or even Peter (Acts 15:13–21). Barnabas is also called an apostle (Acts 14:14), and his apostleship was recognized by the church at the same time as Paul's. Paul also speaks of Andronicus and Junias as being "outstanding among the apostles, and they were in Christ before I was" (Romans 16:7 NIV).

ONLY TWELVE?

Many have argued that there were only twelve apostles, but as Bishop Lightfoot points out in his commentary on Galatians, "Neither the canonical scriptures nor the early Christian writings afford sufficient ground for any such limitations of the apostolate." Others have accepted that Paul, Barnabas and James were apostles, but still claim that the apostolic ministry is a thing of the past. Howard Snyder writes:

Some have argued that apostles no longer exist today, but this conclusion runs counter to Biblical evidence... Nothing in Paul's treatment of spiritual gifts suggests that he was describing a pattern for the early church only. Quite the opposite. For Paul, the church is a growing, grace-filled body, and apostles are a permanent part of that body's life.

(Howard A. Snyder, *Community of the King*, IVP, 1977)

Many who have reluctantly conceded that the gift of tongues might still be with us have continued to dismiss it by saying it is only the least of the gifts. The apostolic gift, if it is for today, certainly cannot be similarly shrugged off. After Jesus ascended, He gave apostles, prophets, evangelists and pastor/teachers to equip the saints until the church is brought to full maturity (Ephesians 4:12–13). We must not miss the vital word "until". Few would argue that the church has reached its full stature, and if any of these grace gifts are missing, we will not reach God's intended goal.

WE HAVE EPISTLES, WHO NEEDS APOSTLES?

It has been suggested that apostles are no longer needed today because we have the Bible. The New Testament letters of the original apostles are enough. Any Bible teacher can expound these great truths.

Some of our greatest teachers have indeed expounded the epistles with extraordinary life and power. However, the tragic fact is that instead of producing a mature church, "joined and held together by every joint with which it is equipped, when each part is working properly" (Ephesians 4:16, ESV), they have produced preaching centres with huge congregations that disintegrate when the gifted preacher is removed from the scene.

That does not mean we should despise great Bible teachers. Far from it! But what is our goal in building the church? Surely it is that in the end we have a mature expression of the body of Christ. The saints are not only to know sound doctrine, but are also to be equipped for works of service. They have to find their particular gifts and contributions to church life and should be encouraged to function in them. All the gifts of the ascended Christ are needed to reach this maturity. As Peter T. O'Brien argues in his commentary, "The presence of gifted persons within the body makes us dependent on one another, and as every Christian fully utilises his or her gifts for the growth of the body, divine fullness will be experienced" (Peter T. O'Brien, *The Letter to the Ephesians*, The

Pillar New Testament Commentary, Eerdmans, 1999).

The apostles of the early church did not fulfil only the role of writing the inspired New Testament. (Only a few of the apostles actually wrote our New Testament, helped by others such as Luke, who wrote more New Testament than anyone, yet claimed no apostolic calling). Just as in the Old Testament there were prophets who contributed nothing to Scripture, yet fulfilled a genuine prophetic ministry, so there were New Testament apostles who never gave us a line of Scripture, yet had a vital role to fulfil among the churches of their day.

MASTER BUILDER

One of the distinctive features of apostles is that they are master builders and foundation layers (1 Corinthians 3:10). Paul did not regard his apostleship as a position in the church hierarchy. He did not see himself at the top of a corporate pyramid; he was not a chief executive in a complicated church superstructure.

Paul had a stewardship from God: he was to proclaim the unfathomable riches of Christ and bring people to an assured understanding of what it is to be in Christ and have Christ in them. This was the burden of apostolic doctrine. Paul did not wonder what he would preach from town to town; he had a body of doctrine to deliver. He knew when the saints had grasped it, and he knew when they had drifted from it. He could see the creeping death of legalism moving over one congregation and warned another against the subtle dangers of mystic Gnosticism. Modern churches still need the authoritative word that will set them free from legalism, super-spirituality and other dangers.

Many an evangelical has thought liberalism to be the great enemy, not recognizing other, perhaps more subtle, foes. Legalism, for instance, can look like commendable zeal; but Paul had no hesitation in calling it another gospel, not to be received even from an angel. How many in the average evangelical church are deeply assured that they have been delivered from sin, have died to the law, and are free from all condemnation? Apostolic doctrine handled with apostolic authority and insight is desperately needed.

Often we are blind to our own faults or shortcomings. Sometimes wrong emphases can enter in, hardly noticed by a local church focusing on itself. Spiritual coldness, doctrinal off-centredness, or incorrect practice can unobtrusively become part of a church's life.

One of God's great provisions to safeguard His church from going astray is a continuing apostolic ministry. Apostles, essentially travelling men, are able to bring objectivity to their appraisal of a local church's condition. For instance, although the church in Thessalonica was in many ways exemplary, Paul wrote to the believers there that he longed to see them so he could supply what was lacking in their faith (1 Thessalonians 3:10). Others, such as the saints in Corinth, Galatia and Colossae, had much for which to thank God in Paul's care of their churches.

FEELING THE NEED

To illustrate further, if a local church, for instance, has not only received an attitude of legalism but has actually built some of its church structure around it, who has the authority to bring correction? The elders often feel trapped within the framework and long for an outside voice to proclaim the way forward authoritatively. Indeed, it is very often the elders who most feel the need for the apostolic ministry. At a recent ministers' conference I addressed, it was acknowledged that, even if they could not yet see all the scriptural basis for apostolic ministry, the ministers personally felt the need for such figures to arise to help them in their leadership of the congregation.

Traditional churches are feeling the pressures of new life. Charismatic gifts are emerging; a desire for freer worship is being expressed. How are the leaders to proceed? Many are facing such issues and do not know which way to turn. Conferences for like-minded pastors will not provide the full answer, nor will charismatic organizations. God's way is to give apostles and prophets. He has simply appointed servants with different gifts to do different jobs.

Paul's authority was not derived from a special title or office. It was the fruit of two things: first, the grace of God in calling and equipping him with a particular gift as an apostle; and secondly, the working relationship he had with any particular church or individual. For example, Paul's fatherly relationship towards the churches in Corinth, Galatia and Thessalonica is plain to see. He wrote to the Corinthians, "in Christ Jesus I became your father through the gospel" (1 Corinthians 4:15). He rejoiced in their lives and their love, and wept over their failures and shortcomings. As their father he lovingly and forthrightly claimed spiritual authority among them.

When writing to the church at Rome, however, Paul's style was different. He felt free to communicate, but he did not adopt the same approach he had used with other churches. He had not yet seen the Roman church face to face; they were not his "children in the Lord".

ELDERSHIP APPOINTMENT

Paul's fatherly care for the church was also demonstrated in his concern that they have local leaders. The appointment of elders was an important aspect of his church building programme. The Holy Spirit selected elders, but they received public recognition through the laying on of hands by the apostles or their delegates.

Modern churches have often resorted to electing their leaders, but those elected into office can similarly be voted out of office, so the temptation to be a man-pleaser is considerable. Appointed by the congregation, such leaders are accountable to the congregation. When there is no anointing, democracy is probably the safest form of church government. But when God begins to give anointed leadership, democracy must make room for Him to have His way.

In the New Testament the whole matter was far more charismatic, in the word's truest sense. The Spirit-led appointment of elders was an important part of the apostles' foundation-laying ministry. Without the Holy Spirit's guidance, we resort to man-made structures with varying degrees of success, even leading to manifest disaster. In recent days some have even found it difficult to elect new leaders because differences of opinion in the congregation make the required majority hard to find. Where there is no acknowledgment of charismatic gifts of leadership, we are bound to hit problems.

Wise master builders will not select elders of their own choice in an arbitrary way. They will observe the way in which men have earned the respect and love of the people and are displaying the fact that God Himself has appointed them. The laying on of hands then becomes an outward acknowledgment of what God has done by His Spirit. It is also a time of further impartation of spiritual grace for eldership.

REGIONS BEYOND

Another major aspect of the work of apostles is breaking new ground with the gospel. Paul was always looking for virgin territory where new churches could be built. As he set sail, he inspired existing churches with his outreaching vision.

Paul planned to see the church at Rome on his way to Spain and be helped on his way by them (Romans 15:24); so the Roman church was drawn into the apostle's missionary thrust into Spain. Members of Paul's team kept the churches informed of his movements, and kept him informed of the churches' progress. Young Timothys were caught up in the world vision and were trained in the apostolic team. They learned in living situations.

So, just as local pastors reproduce after their kind at home, apostles reproduce after their kind while on their apostolic journeys. Soon Timothy or Titus could be sent with Paul's full blessing to do the job he himself would have done. Thus the work was multiplied.

As a result of their travels the apostles not only opened up new areas but brought a sense of unity to the work of God at large. Because of this unity, Paul was able, through his contacts, to bring not only spiritual help but also material help to churches in need. The poor in Jerusalem, for example, were helped by the churches Paul visited elsewhere. It is clear from the New Testament that God never intended local churches to be isolated. Through their relationships with the unifying work of an apostle, they are caught up in an international fellowship and in the worldwide spreading of the gospel. People in local churches who have no larger vision are often tempted to become inward-looking and negative; but where there is global vision and the stimulus of news from other growing churches, there is a strong desire for expansion.

WHAT DO YOU WANT TO BUILD?

Can we do without apostles? The answer very much depends on what we are aiming to build. If we want simply to preserve the status quo, certainly we can cope without them. If we want a nice, cosy, charismatic house group or a safe institutional church enjoying a little renewal now and then, we can find some of our hopes fulfilled. But if we want to see the church come to the fullness of the stature of Christ, to a mature man, it is essential for all the gifted people mentioned in Ephesians 4 to have their full place in our church life.

How do apostles emerge? Like evangelists and prophets, by the sovereign choice and anointing of God. Thus there is no apostolic succession, nor is there any one training ground that produces all these leaders. Paul emerged from a background different from that of the other apostles, but needed the assurance that those he knew to be apostles before him recognized his calling and would extend the right hand of fellowship to him, which, in fact, they were happy to do (Galatians 2:9).

If apostles are only to work on virgin soil where Christ has not been named, is there any room in the West for apostles today? Christ is certainly "named" throughout the Western nations, but we all know in what way many of the 90 per cent outside our churches use that name.

CHURCH PLANTING

The fact remains that if we are to see the tide turn in the nations, we need to plant a great number of new churches – churches that are healthy, powerful communities built firmly on God's word and relevant to modern society. Such new churches *are* being planted today, motivated and served by apostolic ministry. In addition, churches that have been in existence for many years often seek the aid of this ministry to help them through barriers they have found impossible to penetrate on their own.

Several Old Testament books describe the work of restoration that took place after the Babylonian captivity. We can identify wholly with Ezra and Nehemiah in the rebuilding programme and also derive great encouragement from Haggai and Zechariah as we rebuild the ruins of church life. Like Ezra, we need to recover fully the place of the Scriptures; and like Nehemiah, we find that much rubbish needs to be removed. Great tenacity is called for to see the recovery work completed.

NOT IMPOSED AUTHORITY

One part of the role of contemporary apostles is to bring the measuring line to church life to see if it matches up with biblical standards. That is not to say they will arrive uninvited at any local church to declare their judgments. If the mighty apostle Paul was not automatically recognized by all as an apostle, and if his presence was regarded by some as unimpressive and contemptible, we can be sure that far lesser apostles would find it very difficult to impose their authority, or, indeed, to be recognized at all!

Modern apostles will be regarded by some as simply brothers or preachers, while to others they function as apostles. That presents no problem; it is not unlike the attitude Christians might have towards local pastors/teachers from other churches in their area. Uninvited apostles cannot impose their authority in other churches; nor should it be their desire to do so. They will, however, happily respond to requests from church elders who reach out for their help.

Modern apostles make no claims to infallibility, and surely our understanding is that only God's word is infallible, not the actions of even New Testament apostles. Hence we see Paul having to correct Peter for his wrongful action in connection with the circumcision advocates (Galatians 1:11–14). Surely modern apostles would not put themselves above the apostle Peter. We can rejoice that we now have the completed Scriptures, not to *replace* spiritual gifts or the Ephesians 4 ministries, but as a means by which we may *test* them to be assured that they are of God.

APOSTOLIC TEAMS

Like Paul, modern apostles will find they cannot work alone. As the work multiplies they will draw colleagues to their side. We have coined the phrase "apostolic team", but we must be careful not to suggest something official by that title. There is no such thing as "team status". Paul sometimes moved with some men, sometimes with others. They did not thereby claim a peculiar position as "team members". The arrangement was purely functional and very fluid.

In sending Timothy, Paul was confident that he would remind them of "my ways which are in Christ, just as I teach everywhere in every church" (1 Corinthians 4:17). The men who travelled with Paul, and who were sent to and from him, multiplied the ministry. Their relationship with Paul provided a setting in which they no doubt developed their own "ways in Christ"; they would keep a strong dependence on Paul, but would also develop their own special contribution.

Some men travelling with an apostle will be like Barnabas – former local leaders who have proved their worth at a flourishing home church that is now sufficiently secure to release them. Others will be young men like Timothy, who not only commend themselves to the apostle, but also have excellent relationships with local elders, who sense the hand of God upon them and release them gladly to the larger work.

CARE FOR THE CHURCHES

So we have a company of men who know that their prime calling is no longer to one particular local work – though their roots are there – but to the church at large. Whereas once they had the care of a local flock, they begin to develop a care for the churches – plural (2 Corinthians 11:28).

Within the so-called "team" there will be embryonic apostles like Timothy; there will also be those with other gifts – prophets or evangelists, for instance – whose roles will differ, but who find a "team" relationship truly helpful in keeping them from being isolated and vulnerable.

It is important to see that prophets, evangelists and pastors/ teachers have different ministries and therefore will not try to bring to a local church what in the end only an apostle can bring. There is a danger, when a man moves into a different area of gifting, that he will be ineffective, resulting in frustration and insecurity. For instance, when trying to represent the apostle, the pastor who is not truly apostolic may tend to hold back where he should be decisive. Failing to recognize fundamental problems in a church, he may continue to encourage and build up the people when really some "tearing down" must take place first. His gifts of teaching and caring are best used when a good foundation is already laid in terms of doctrine, practice and eldership. Like a dentist who knows there is more decay in a tooth which must be removed before a filling can be added, the apostle will insist on basic changes in doctrine, style, structure or leadership personnel before simply building up the people with encouraging ministry.

Alternatively a pastor may compensate for lack of apostolic anointing by undue legalism and "going by the book" which promotes a system instead of life. The prophet will excite activity, but will tend to breed insecurity when he is not joined to an apostle. The evangelist will gather many people, but will not build them together. As a team bound with an apostle in love and mutual respect, they become a mighty force in the kingdom of God.

Paul's travels took him across national borders from country to country. Often he was separated for long periods of time from churches he had fathered. By modern means of communication and travel, 21st-century apostles and their colleagues can be in much closer contact with the churches they serve. By telephone and e-mails we can reach around the world in moments; by motorways we can travel miles for an evening's meeting; by jet plane we can circle the globe in a few hours; by books and online links we can speak when we are not even present.

There are no international barriers to apostolic ministry, and, in fact, at one time the company travelling with Paul comprised men from several nations (Acts 20:4). Apostolic ministry transcends nationalism and does not attempt to superimpose one nation's culture on another. Some travelling ministers will count it their joy to stimulate the development of emerging apostles and prophets in other nations, and then to step back to let them fulfil their calling, as Barnabas did with Paul. God will thus raise up Antioch churches all over the world – churches of far-reaching vision that release fresh apostolic and prophetic ministry.

Paul anticipated that local churches would grow in grace and release him to ever-increasing spheres of influence. Churches failing to develop in maturity often meant that the apostle Paul had to delay breaking into new territory in order to bring correction to their internal failures. So apostolic advance was intimately linked with local church development. Paul very much wanted to preach the gospel to regions beyond and argued, "your growing faith will mean the expansion of our sphere of action" (2 Corinthians 10:15 J. B. Phillips).

Healthy local churches release the dynamic of apostolic advance and result in multiplied new churches being planted and new nations being penetrated.

As one apostolic team develops and grows it can result in other apostolic ministries emerging. Paul will send Timothy who knows Paul's ways in Christ and can faithfully represent him. Other men will similarly act on his behalf as Titus did in Crete. No doubt as time went by, these men who initially were delegated to represent Paul would themselves emerge carrying their own sense of calling and gifting, again gathering around themselves apostolic teams that could multiply ministry.

The Bible promises that there will be no end to the increase of the government of Christ. His kingdom will grow until the promise made to Abraham – that all the families of the earth will be blessed

– is fulfilled. Spirit-filled churches provide the key to the advance of the kingdom of God. It is my longing that they will be multiplied in nation after nation until all the unreached people groups are reached for the glory of God.

BIBLIOGRAPHY

F. F. Bruce, *Hebrews*, NICNT, Eerdmans, 1990

D. A. Carson, *A Call to Spiritual Reformation*, Baker Book House, 1992

Samuel Chadwick, *The Path of Prayer*, Hodder & Stoughton, 1931

Eileen Crossman, *Mountain Rain*, OMF Books, 1982

Jack Deere, *Surprised by the Power of the Spirit*, Kingsway, 1994

Gordon Fee, *God's Empowering Presence*, Hendrickson, 1994

Gordon Fee, *Paul, the Spirit and the People of God*, Hodder & Stoughton, 1997

Jack Hayford, *The Church on the Way*, Zondervan, 1985

William Hendriksen, *The Gospel of John*, Banner of Truth, 1959

Philip Hughes, *Second Epistle to the Corinthians*, NICNT, Eerdmans, 1962

C. S. Lewis, *Reflections on the Psalms*, Harcourt Brace & World, 1958

J. B. Lightfoot, *St Paul's Epistle to the Galatians*, Macmillan, 1981

Dr Martyn Lloyd-Jones, *Joy Unspeakable*, Kingsway, 1984

Dr Martyn Lloyd-Jones, *Westminster Record*, Vol. 43, No. 9

Douglas Moo, *The Epistle to the Romans*, NICNT, Eerdmans, 1996

Peter T. O'Brien, *The Letter to the Ephesians*, The Pillar New Testament Commentary, Eerdmans, 1999.

J. I. Packer, *Knowing God*, Hodder & Stoughton, 1973

J. I. Packer, *A Passion for Holiness*, Crossway, 1992

A. W. Pink, *The Attributes of God*, Baker Book House, 1975

John Piper, *Desiring God*, IVP, 1986 (also Multnomah, 1986)

Charles Simpson, *The Challenge to Care*, Vine Books, 1986

Howard A. Snyder, *Community of the King*, IVP, 1977

R. C. Sproul, *The Holiness of God*, Tyndale House, 1985

R. C. Sproul, *The Soul's Quest for God*, Tyndale House, 1992

C. H. Spurgeon, *Autobiography*, Banner of Truth, 1962

John Stott, *The Message of Acts*, The Bible Speaks Today, IVP, 1990

John Stott, *The Message of Galatians*, The Bible Speaks Today, IVP, 1986

John Stott, *One People*, Falcon Books, 1969

John Stott, "Quenching the Holy Spirit", *Westminster Record*, September 1969

B. B. Warfield, *Counterfeit Miracles*, Banner of Truth, 1972

Rob Warner, *21st Century Church*, Hodder & Stoughton, 1993

Bishop Westcott, *The Gospel According to St John*, James Clarke, 1958

Christopher Wright, *Deuteronomy*, NIBC, Hendrickson/Paternoster, 1996

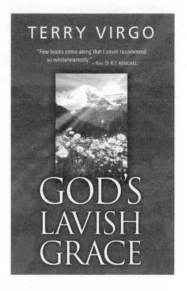